Mary Clark Norris

Much Stronger Than My Struggles

He Pulled Me Through

The Strength to Overcome

Doubt and Frustration in the Midst

of Turmoil and Confusion

HIS GLORY
CREATIONS PUBLISHING LLC

His Glory Creations Publishing, LLC

Wendell, North Carolina

ISBN: 978-1-7327227-7-4

King James Version (KJV) Scripture references are used with permission from Zondervan via Biblegateway.com

We hope you enjoy this book from His Glory Creations Publishing, LLC. Our goal is to provide high-quality, thought provoking books that connect to your real needs and challenges. For more information on other books and products, go to www.hisglorycreationspublishing.com

Printed in the United States of America

In Memory of my Beautiful and Loving Mother

Nancy Clark

"Gone Too Soon"

Mom, I wish you were still here with me to witness my life and share in all my plans and experiences I have had with writing. Nevertheless, I know that you are here with me in spirit. I never would have imagined that writing a book or books would be something that I could do let alone, enjoy. Writing has brought me so much comfort and peace that I could have never imagined in my wildest dream. I know now more than ever; God has a plan for my life and besides he has already confirmed it more than 7 times.

Mom, you have always encouraged me to dream BIG and reach high and as you would lovingly say, "Jesus is at the top!" I hope that I make you proud of me and in my stance of walking in the will of God and not be moved. I am who I am today because you were my mother and I am grateful to God for him lending you to me for such a time to call you, "Mama."

I would like to thank you for always instilling in me that I could do anything that I put my mind to. You have poured the Word of God in me through scriptures and prayers that I can do all things through Christ that strengthens me. Because of your love, I am equipped to tackle any obstacle that may come to try to discourage and diminish my faith. As you have always reminded me, no matter what, why, when and where, God will never forsake you. Never! Thank you for your sincere love that will always lead and guide me as the Holy Spirit led and guided you for many years. **God Bless You Mama Nana #RIP**

Dedication

This book is also dedicated to my DAD, Otis Clark, Sr. Thank you for pushing me to be my very best in everything that I do. You have labored and prayed for me when I had no strength or faith to even pray for myself. Thank you for the love and support that you have always given me. When I was a little girl, I remember the countless times that you made sacrifices for our family without ever hesitating. Your love and guidance have pushed me to be strong and to stand up for what I believe. I am who I am because of your love and steady commitment you have for God and our family.

I thought dedicating this book to you is so befitting because you have always encouraged me to believe that as a family, we were always stronger than our struggles. Thank You for those words which have kept me and always pushed me to my next level in God. You continue to encourage me to push beyond the veil and see Jesus and not my situation. I have always remembered that and will always remember the reason I have come this far by faith. I cannot turn around now.

Out of, *all* the things that we have experienced growing up as a family; truly, I have never seen the righteous forsaken nor his seed begging for bread. You have always promised me that God would take care of us even when the going gets tough, and the tough gets going. This book reminds me of the many times you have spoken so prophetically over my life in the most powerful of ways but so effortless. You have encouraged me not to question the plans of God for my life but to move beyond the boundaries and restrictions of others to see the fullness of His Glory in me. And daily, you continue to speak to my spirit and provide me with powerful bible quotes and scriptures that have breathed life back into me when I was dying spiritually. I love you Daddy! You will always be the love of my life, and I will always be your baby girl.

This book is dedicated to my Adopted Parents, Bishop Zack, and Mary Clyde Rogers. Also, to The Clark Family and The Rogers Family. My Forever Loves.

This book is also dedicated to a very special person and friend, Angie Andrews whom from day one has supported and believed in me and encouraged me that I can do this thing called *writing a book*. From the beginning of time, you read my first manuscript and assured me that it was *good stuff*. Thanks for believing in me and my vision to write. You continue to push me and motivate me every day to keep going. I believe that one day, like you always said; "we are going to get that bus." #LOL

Foreword

I AM DELIGHTED to write this foreword, not only because Mary Clark Norris is my adopted sister, but also because I deeply admire Mary's passion and drive to push beyond the layers of what she can see and visualize what we sometimes believe is the "impossible." Nevertheless; we know that it is God who makes all things possible and all things brand new. Mary's determination and willpower to succeed is contagious. It is that same drive that makes Mary not accept the mediocre or status quo while building her brand. Although life success can be measured in many ways, it is the determined individual that refuses to throw in the towel on their goals, visions, and dreams that makes a dedicated and successful person. And that person is whom I am proud to call my sister, Mary Clark Norris.

Life is a journey and no matter the journey, it is your drive that forces you to leap to higher heights and unleveled grounds. This is what I believe Mary has allowed us to see through the writing of this book. Despite some of the hardships and trials that she has experienced in her own personal life, Mary continues to motivate others to be strong and courageous as they press through the jungle of their past and present and find their true purpose.

This book is a testament to me because it challenges me not to give up during life storms and struggles but seek beyond my own fears, insecurities and uncertainties as I pursue my destiny. Although this has always been difficult for me, I too, had to challenge myself to embrace the pain and life experiences by living outside of my fears and not allowing the hurt to consume me and my mind. I have learned that the reality of life and death at an early age can shape one's life for a lifetime. How to understand it all or to know what it all means can be a question that is constantly asked over and over again. Even then, we may never know the answer or better yet, the truth.

All I can remember is that one lonely and dark day; I became consumed with hatred and fear that filled my heart and splattered my mind daily. But what would one expect when you give a teenage boy a gun, leave him alone 10 thousand miles away from home to fight for his country? Each day and many times a day death became my friend, and I had no one there to explain it all to me. Sitting in a wet fox hole, crying for my mother, my only hope was to go home. It was my first Christmas without my family, and I was devastated by the impact this situation had on me. My thought was "this can't be real, no it can't be," but it was, and I knew it right when I heard the loud noise, a bomb that blasted right in front of us. Afraid and naïvely, I screamed, Jones! Jones! Jones was gone. There was nothing I could do to save him. What will I tell his mother, I thought to myself? I promised to bring him back home with me. And now, I was faced with the task to not only bring my best friend back home but bring him back home in a body bag. My heart dropped, and there was nothing more that I could do to stop this anger from rising up in my heart. "Why" is the question that I asked everyone around me but nobody could answer me and help me to find the reason for my agony? Bitterness and rage occupied the space in my soul because I never could understand the level of pain that rose upon me and would stay for a long time before I received my total healing and deliverance.

So, yes, it was my struggles that saved my life. It allowed me to see myself in my own mirror for the very first time. Through it all, I know that God was with me and allowed me to triumph over the enemy and his tactics against me one more time and I am thankful for his love and protection.

So, I applaud Mary for writing this great book that has encouraged and inspired me and helped push me out of my comfort zone. I have learned in reading this book that I too am Much Stronger than My Struggles.

Jimmie Gregory Rogers, Sr.

Table of Contents

INTRODUCTION

FIRST AND FOREMOST, You Must Understand that God is the Author of your Strength and the Founder of Your Faith. When you rely on the strength of God and the power of the Holy Spirit, you will begin to experience a life overflowing with milk and honey. That's the "exceedingly and abundantly" above all you could ever ask or think kind of blessing. It is important to have faith in God for everything and not depend on your own understanding and intellect to get you through the hard times. It is our struggles that make us stronger and continue to push us beyond the veil to see something that we have never seen. We must put our trust in the Almighty God and know that he will deliver on every promise and every Word that proceeds out of his mouth. God will never forsake his people even when it looks like the odds are against you and that you are outnumbered. His ways are not our ways; neither are his thoughts like ours. But one thing, you can be rest assured, because He knows your name, and he sees and knows all the oppositions you are confronted with by your enemies. Though, there are weapons being formed against you daily, I am a believer, it will not prosper, and of course, it will not work. The King James Version of 2nd Corinthians sums it up like this: For the weapons of our warfare are not carnal, but mighty through God to the pulling down of strongholds. Casting down imaginations, and every high thing that exalteth itself against the knowledge of God and bringing into captivity every thought to the obedience of Christ.

Your true identity begins in Him. We have to cast down everything that is not like God and become who we are in Christ through our relationship with him. Seeing yourself the way God sees you and then acknowledging that you are more than a conqueror through Jesus Christ is a testament to many. When you don't know who you are you will begin to struggle with the person that you see in your own mirror. The mix identity issues can be the downfall of your many blessings and you getting to your appointed assignments in God. You cannot allow your struggle to rob your peace of mind. You must defeat the enemy with your praise and your push. Your struggle is the push to your next and upcoming breakthrough. You have to remember that you are much stronger and bigger than the giant that stands in front of you. **So, Go Forth, Child of God! On Your Mark, Get Ready, Get Set… NOW PUSH!**

Chapter One

I have been young, and now am old; yet have I not seen the righteous
forsaken, nor his seed begging bread.

Psalms 107:25 (KJV)

Never Forsaken

How many times have we faced situations in our lives that have left us
feeling lonely and forsaken? The enemy's plan is to take our peace and
destroy our purpose. The enemy sees your strong pursuit, and he knows
that this time you will win and recover all. Therefore, he has tried to corner
you and pressuring you into believing that God is not going to help you
fight in this battle. The enemy wants you to believe that the game is over
when the game has just begun. Greatness is inside of you, and he knows
that too, but he also knows that God has begun a good work in you and
promises to perform it until the day you die. This is what causes him to
flinch and angle to stop your praise and hinder your breakthrough. Every
time he sees you winning his scheme is to distract you and take your joy.

Believe me, the work is working in you, and this has caused the enemy
to take another look at things and change his approach. That's okay too
because now God is about to change his approach on the enemy. God sees
every hurt and broken place in you. He sees your hands are about to come

down because you are too weak to keep them up. He knows that the enemy is fighting against your home and you and your husband's marriage is hanging on by a thread. He knows that the enemy is now coming for your children in order to get to you. God knows that you lost that home and your car was repossessed last night. He knows that you are dealing with suicidal thoughts and depression. He knows that your health has taken a turn for the worst. He sees your tears and all your struggles. He knows that you are just at the brink of losing your mind. He knows that Woman. Man.

But, do you want to know what else he knows? He knows that although you are down now, it is just temporary. He knows that your weeping and howling will only last for a night. He knows that his Joy is coming, and it doesn't have to just show up in the morning, but now. He knows that although weapons are forming against you and your family, they will not prosper. He knows that Greater is on the inside of you and all you have to do is tap into it. He knows that all of what you are going through right now looks like a setback but actually it is a set-up for your comeback. The enemy knows that your breakthrough is on the way. He knows that, and he knows you. But God wants you to remain faithful and trust in him through it all. God is not going to flee the scene and run like some convict. He is in it to win it and so should you.

The Word tells us to: Be ye steadfast always abounding in the works of the Lord knowing that your labor is not in vain. God will pull you through and see to it that you will prosper in this season because you are pregnant with purpose. So, remember, it doesn't matter what it looks like from the angle in which you stand, God is still God, and he is still good. He is our Shepherd, our King, and our Great Majesty. When I stumble, he leads me beside the still waters to rest in him. He then restores my soul so that I can strengthen my faith and keep walking with him. Afterward, he leads me in the path of righteousness so that I will not fear but have hope and endure the testing of times. He is the beginning of our beginning and the end of our ending. Like so many times, he pulled Job through, and he will pull you through too. You are never forsaken!

Psalms 23: 1-6 (KJV)

The LORD is my shepherd; I shall not want. He maketh me to lie down in green pastures: he leadeth me beside the still waters. He restoreth my soul: he leadeth me in the paths of righteousness for his name's sake. Yea, though I walk through the valley of the shadow of death, I will fear no evil: for thou art with me; thy rod and thy staff they comfort me. Thou preparest a table before me in the presence of mine enemies: thou anointest my head with oil; my cup runneth over. Surely goodness and mercy shall follow me all the days of my life: and I will dwell in the house of the LORD forever.

In times like these, it is easier to get intimidated and feel stricken but yet forsaken because of the added pressure to win. But God will not leave you nor forsake you even during the most pivotal time of your life. He promised to be with you even until the end of the earth and through every hardship and setback. You must remember you are on the winning side and you are destined to win. The gifts and talents are already placed on the inside of you. Now, it is time for you to stir up the gifts and allow God to make and mold you into his own image. From the time of inception, you were born to win which means everything attached to you wins also. Your ancestors have been winning for years. You are a son and a daughter of The Most High King of Kings and the Prince of Peace. You are entitled to the throne. You were born to shake up the enemy's camp and destroy his territory. The anointing was birthed on the inside of you when you were in your mother's womb. You kicked and screamed because of the power and the authority that was already upon your life. No, you will not be defeated! It doesn't matter what it looks like right now from the bottom looking up, you are not forsaken, and you will not take down. Why? Because it is in your DNA to win and not quit. You will conquer all. Quitters never win anything! So, stick to what you have believed from the very beginning, and that is, with God all things are possible. It is no time to give up and quit on God. You are at the brink of your breakthrough, and the enemy knows it too. That is why his aim is to push you over the edge. You must be determined to win and not get distracted during this race. Run with patience and be diligent during every test and trial that comes upon you. Go the extra mile even when you get weak and are persuaded to give up by the schemes of the enemy. Remember, you are a Champion, and you are already predestined to prosper. You can do it, and all you have to do is keep pushing and never ever quit. I am reminded of the verse in Philippians that says… I can do all things through Christ which strengthens me. The Greater is already in you. Therefore, you have what it takes to withstand in this fight. Just know, the enemy cannot stand you, but he can do nothing to stop you either. Because this race is not given to the swift or the battle to the strong but to the ones, who hold out and endures to the end. If you are willing to fight to the finish, you have already won. Well Done!

2 Timothy 1: 6-9 (KJV)

Wherefore I put thee in remembrance that thou stir up the gift of God, which is in thee by the putting on of my hands. For God hath not given us the spirit of fear; but of power, and of love, and of a sound mind. Be not thou therefore ashamed of

the testimony of our Lord, nor of me his prisoner: but be thou partaker of the afflictions of the gospel according to the power of God; Who hath saved us, and called us with an holy calling, not according to our works, but according to his own purpose and grace, which was given us in Christ Jesus before the world began.

The Bible reminds us that we war not after the flesh but after the spirit. The problem is that we fight against the wrong people. The truth is that this battle is not against man or woman. The real battle is against Satan, the devil. That disgusted and lousy bum of the enemy that you continue to allow back in your lifetime and time again. The one who on many occasions, has stolen your joy and destroyed your peace of mind. So, my problem is not with you but the devil that works in you. You must not allow Satan to confuse you and get you to think that your neighbor is your enemy. Your real enemy is the one who has deceived you in thinking that your neighbor is your enemy. Your neighbor could be mad with you and not speaking to you, but it is the enemy that has plagued your neighbor's mind to war against you and your family.

St. Matthew 6:14-15 (KJV)

For if ye forgive men their trespasses, your heavenly Father will also forgive you: But if ye forgive not men their trespasses, neither will your Father forgive your trespasses.

Forgiveness can be very difficult. People can be so cruel and ugly by doing things that are offensive to others. I remember the much younger me when I was fuming with this girl because I felt that she was very mean to me and was out to destroy my life. And to be honest with you, she probably

5

was. Yes, her actions towards me were evil and she was a big bully too. I seriously wanted to hate her. And to be honest with you, I probably secretly did. But then, one day, God reminded me who I was in him. I am created to glorify God and him only will I serve. I had to embrace his Glory and allow him to heal my heart. Having an unforgiving heart can lead to bitterness, and I knew those behaviors would keep me from receiving God's grace. A heart that is bitter can hinder us from loving people. And we all know what the Bible tells us about the importance of loving others. Well, in case you do not know. The Bible says in I John 4:7-8: Beloved, let us love one another: for love is of God, and every one that loveth is born of God and knoweth God. He that loveth not knoweth not God; for God is love. That scripture reads plain and very clear. There is no deviating or adding on or taking off the Word of God. Love is Love. Either you have love, or you don't. There are no in-betweens. I had to face the facts and put things in perspective for my life at that moment. It was not easy, but it was a part of God's plan for me to be transformed and renewed in my mind. I want to speak into somebody's life right now who are battling with the Spirit of unforgiveness, let it go. Unless you change your mindset, things in your life will never change. You must begin to see things differently before change takes place. Transformation begins with a changed mind. Once you have made up your mind and heart to love, there is no stopping you. It is your duty to live true to yourself, with authenticity. *Love is Freedom. Love is Forever. Love is Freewill. Love is for you. And Love is for me. If you want it, you can have it…..just love. Because love can heal the land.*

I Corinthians 13: 1-8 (KJV)

Though I speak with the tongues of men and of angels, and have not charity, I am become as sounding brass, or a tinkling cymbal. And though I have the gift of prophecy, and

understand all mysteries, and all knowledge; and though I have all faith, so that I could remove mountains, and have not charity, I am nothing. And though I bestow all my goods to feed the poor, and though I give my body to be burned, and have not charity, it profiteth me nothing. Charity suffereth long, and is kind; charity envieth not; charity vaunteth not itself, is not puffed up, Doth not behave itself unseemly, seeketh not her own, is not easily provoked, thinketh no evil; Rejoiceth not in iniquity, but rejoiceth in the truth; Beareth all things, believeth all things, hopeth all things, endureth all things. Charity never faileth: but whether there be prophecies, they shall fail; whether there be tongues, they shall cease; whether there be knowledge, it shall vanish away.

So, one day, God begin to charge me with studying the Bible and being consistent in reading and studying the Word of God. I begin to seek for peace in the Word, and I found out that God will bring healing through his Word. I needed God's peace to help sustain me while I was in a lonely and destitute but troublesome place. The ill-feelings that had built up in me toward that girl were awful. I knew there had to be a change in me, so I begin to seek God for his management and guidance to break through the chains that had me bound. That day, God spoke to me and told me who was my real enemy.....Satan. God started to deal with my heart, and he spoke deeply within my spirit to wake up so that I could see his truth. After the revelation and conviction that day, I was so ashamed of my actions toward this girl. I purely cried of shame and embarrassment of how I allowed the devil to use me and misguide my thoughts. I am sure I am not the only one who has allowed the enemy to use them. We know better but, at that moment, I allowed the enemy to deceive me and try to make me feel powerful behind jealousy, bitterness, and confusion. This is a prime example of a total set-up by the enemy. Jesus says it best when he told Simon Peter that the enemy desire was to have you that he may sift you as wheat. As God warned Peter, he is also warning us today to be watchful and pray that our faith will not fail but that we recognize the works of the enemy and not fall prey to his schemes. At this moment, I can hear the very words recited to me by my mother; *a warning always comes before destruction.* That day, I quickly asked God for his forgiveness. I was able to find peace in my spirit after I forgave the person for the part they played in the matter towards me. You see, I have learned that forgiveness is not about the other person. Forgiveness is about you and me becoming free from all bondages and strongholds. We hold on to things because of selfish and egotistical reasons when the pain only consumes us and breaks our spirit. We are the ones affected by the pain and hurt. We are walking around here all bitter, broken and bruised. We have to know who is fighting against us. We have to realize that we do not battle against flesh and blood or like I said earlier, man or woman. This fight is much bigger than that.

This battle is against the enemy who seeks to take you out and to terminate your planned destiny. The aim is to destroy you and abort the gifts inside of you. If you want to get angry, get angry at the right one. If you want to fight, fight against the right one. Now, you can stop fighting in the streets with guns and killing each other. They are not your enemy! Start fighting in the Spirit. God has already given us weapons to fight. You have to cast down imaginations and strongholds and begin to war in the spirit against anything that tries to exalt itself against God. It is not your neighbor. It is not your co-worker. It is not your family. It's not even me. It is your adversary, that Beelzebub who seeks to immolate you because you are aiming to be great. Know your opponent and know that he has plans for your life, but God has plans for his life too which is to destroy the very purpose of his being. Ask God to order your steps as I did on that day. I remembered that day like it was yesterday. When I forgave that person, I was instantaneously set free. I chose to forgive, and God gracefully has forgiven me in return. What a Mighty and Merciful God we serve.

Ephesians 6: 11-13 (KJV)

Put on the whole armour of God, that ye may be able to stand against the wiles of the devil. For we wrestle not against flesh and blood, but against principalities, against powers, against the rulers of the darkness of this world, against spiritual wickedness in high places. Wherefore take unto you the whole armour of God, that ye may be able to withstand in the evil day, and having done all, to stand.

Many times, I have been tempted and tried by the enemy to give up and throw in the towel. I have cried and toiled all night long under pressure by strongholds and grips of the enemy to tear me down. I have faced many obstacles and almost lost my Hope during the test but through it all, I have held on to God's unchanging hands and you can too. God promised to hold us up and not let me fall. Psalms 37 says that though he may stumble, he will not fall, for the Lord upholds him with his hand. God is always showing his love towards us by reassuring his grace and mercy will cover us against the defeat of the enemy. I want to encourage my readers not to faint. I know it will be hard and the storms will blow hard and try to cause us to crumble and fall. Sometimes we may get weak and fall because of the chaos surrounded us but we must get back up and declare the works of the Lord. The Bible says a just man falleth 7 times and gets back up again. This lets me know, it is not how many times you fall but how you get back up. You have to refuse to stay down. You must refuse to lose. If you are his disciple, you can get back up and declare his victory today. God wants to set his people free. All you have to do is abide in the Word and allow the Word to abide in you. The Bible says, you will know the truth, and the truth will set you free. And whom the son has set free is truly free indeed and we claim him to be the Lamb of God. Amen.

Chapter Two

For he commandeth, and raiseth the stormy wind, which lifteth up the waves thereof. They mount up to the heaven, they go down again to the depths: their soul is melted because of trouble. They reel to and fro, and stagger like a drunken man, and are at their wit's end. Then they cry unto the LORD in their trouble, and he bringeth them out of their distresses. He maketh the storm a calm, so that the waves thereof are still. Then are they glad because they be quiet; so he bringeth them unto their desired haven. Oh that men would praise the LORD for his goodness, and for his wonderful works to the children of men!

Psalms 107:25-31 (KJV)

Tossed and Turned

During the last couple of months, it has been reported all over the television about the numerous storms and hurricanes that have come and destroyed major towns and cities all across the world. I was in one of my classes the other night reading CNN News online, and some of the people that were interviewed appeared devastated concerning their loss. The news also stated that some parts of Florida were asked to evacuate immediately because of the category of the hurricane that was approaching. As I continued to read, it talked about the many people who rushed out of their homes to travel to various parts of the world to get away from the storm. Also, I believe I read that many of the people who were asked to evacuate and was leaving had no place to go but would consider shelter for the time being. One family said they had too many family members in their home along with 4 or 5 pets and that it was no way possible they could evacuate their home at the time. It was later noted that the wife said that they would just have to stay and "ride out the storm."

I begin to ponder on that phrase and wonder how many of us when catastrophe strikes our lives that we consider to "ride out the storm." In our lives, there will be so many trials and tribulations that will test our faith. Like any storm, you will be tossed and turned. You will be tried by every storm that you could ever think of to destroy your peace. There will be days when the storm of life will almost get the best of you, and for some, it will. I want you to know that during these times, you must not quit. Do not give in to what was meant to take you out, but just ride out your storm knowing that God is your captain and he will bring you safely to dock. I like the story in the 4th Chapter of St. Mark, where the disciples feared for their lives after which a storm arose, and they summoned Jesus to wake up and save them. There are many people among us who are in their storms today that have allowed fear to control their situations, and have become stunted spiritually. Even when the storm arises, we must stand firm in our faith in God and know that he will take care of us. He promised to never leave you or forsake you and that you can always depend on, his Word. I take joy in knowing even when the worst comes upon my life whether it be in my health or my finances, God's promise is that he will always come through and will not fail me. David said it best when addressing his son, Solomon in I Chronicles 28:20 Be strong and of good courage, and do it: fear not, nor be dismayed: for the LORD God, even my God, will be with thee; he will not fail thee, nor forsake thee, until thou hast finished all the work for the service of the house of the LORD.

St. Mark 4:35-41 (KJV)

And the same day, when the even was come, he saith unto them, Let us pass over unto the other side. And when they had sent away the multitude, they took him even as he was in the ship. And there were also with him other little ships. And there arose a great storm of wind, and the waves beat into the ship, so that it was now full. And he was in the hinder part of the ship, asleep on a pillow: and they awake him, and say unto him, Master, carest thou not that we perish? And he arose, and rebuked the wind, and said unto the sea, Peace, be still. And the wind ceased, and there was a great calm. And he said unto them, Why are ye so fearful? how is it that ye have no faith? And they feared exceedingly, and said one to another, What manner of man is this, that even the wind and the sea obey him?

I am very thankful for the warnings and signs that God gives us daily although it seems pointless at times to many. People continue to ignore and disregard many of the warnings that God has faithfully given to us, but why? Are we not afraid of the outcome and consequences of ignoring the voice of God? We must be mindful when we fail to adhere to the voice of God. Lack of fear and faith in God are strategies that I personally feel are reasoning for society's views and opinions of danger and catastrophes by God. Also, you have to take into account many people who do not believe in God and his existence. So, there view, and understanding is warped. It is so sad that the world has come to this place. The Bible mentions in the 2nd Chapter of Hebrews, the importance of giving heed to the things that we have heard, and that God always sends a warning before destruction. There are all types of warnings sent by all sectors of our society. However, the main warning, I feel we should be aware and mindful of is the end of time warning sent by God.

One day, I was relaxing in my favorite lounger at home and was meditating on what to say to God's people as I prepared for an assignment out of town. As I continued to sit there, I started to think about the overwhelming news on television lately talking about the various places that were destroyed by the many hurricanes both near and far. My heart can only ache and hurt for the many people who have lost their lives and their homes during this disastrous storm. The Lord spoke to me, and he said, "It is water this time, but fire next time." I sprung up in my seat, and I begin to pray for people all over the world. I prayed for the cities and towns that were affected by the storm. I prayed for the many people who have been lost in the physical storm and lost in the spiritual storm of life. People, we have to wake up and see the salvation of the Lord! For time won't be long for his return. I pray that we will all be ready to be lifted up in the sky. My prayers were that we see what is really happening around us and take it as a sign that the Lord is coming soon! There are many signs among us but are we listening is the question? God has allowed us to see his hands in so many of life storms and mishaps and it appears that we are ignoring the signs. What more does God have to do to get us to see him for who He is? We like to say, "I want to be ready when he comes." But what are we doing to prepare for his return? It is one thing to say it but what are we doing so that we can be ready when he comes. The Bible says in St. Matthew Chapter 24 around the 40th verse that two shall be in the field, the one shall be taken and the other left. Then it says two women shall be grinding at the mill; the one shall be taken, and the other left. This brings me to what the Bible says, "No man knows the day or the hour that the Son of Man will appear," so we have to be ready when he comes. We cannot be getting ready, but we have to be ready. God is not going to wait on us to ask for forgiveness and to love our brothers and sisters. Your time to forgive each other is right now. Your time to love your neighbor is right now. Sometimes we hold on to things because of our pride. Well, if you think that the hurt or the lies that someone told you or something someone did to you is bigger than what the Lord is going to do to you on that day if you don't forgive, you better think again, partner. It is up to you to make up your mind and know that this thing is bigger than you anyway.

You have to turn over all that hurt and pain that others have caused you and take it to the Lord in prayer. I promise you. He will handle it like the champ he is. Don't let anything or anyone cause you to miss out on what God is doing in your life because you fail to forgive. I like how the Bible speaks on it in Colossians Chapter 3 in The Message (MSG) Bible. (I want to caution all the non-bible readers). There is a version of the Bible that is called "The Message." Somebody tried to call me out on that. I told them to take several seats in the church and make it a bible study night. Also, there is a King James Version (KJV); New King James Version (NKJV) and the New International Version (NIV), just to name a few. I just want to make sure our non-bible readers are clear and understand about the different versions and languages of the Bible. The Bible speaks simply by saying for us to forgive quickly.

Colossians 3: 12-14 (KJV)

So, chosen by God for this new life of love, dress in the wardrobe God picked out for you: compassion, kindness, humility, quiet strength, discipline. Be even-tempered, content with second place, quick to forgive an offense. Forgive as quickly and completely as the Master forgave you. And

regardless of what else you put on, wear love. It's your basic, all-purpose garment. Never be without it.

In the Bible, it as clear as can be, forgive and quickly forgive again. It is evident in his Word that Jesus knew before we were even created that Forgiveness would be an issue for most of us. Because back in St. Matthew 18th Chapter (KJV), Peter asked Jesus how often should we forgive our brother? Jesus answered and said: I say not unto thee, until seven times: but, until seventy times seven. We show love when we are able to forgive others as Christ has forgiven us. It is the love of the father that helps us to forgive and wear this garment in a way that shows love to everyone we meet.

Several years ago, I thought I was wearing this garment of love as Christ has instructed me to do. I fell into a situation and found out the love of Jesus was not where I wanted it to be, and God was not pleased with me. I quickly confessed my sin (lack of love) and repented and asked God for His Love to embrace me as I would embrace others. Sometimes it can be hard to love others after you have been hurt and scarred. But I often times have to remind myself that it is not about me, but about God. I had to learn this. When we go through problems with others whether it is finding a way to love them or forgive them, you have to remember not to make it about you. If you make it about you, you will find so many reasons not to forgive or love that person. But when you make it about God it becomes easy because the question is brought up, what would Jesus do? The love of the father is so unmeasurable and true. Knowing and understanding God's love for me, allows me to understand my love for others. That true and agape love that is long lasting and forgiving. The more I know Jesus, the more I know myself, and that feeling is all too refreshing. Love is Kind. Love is Peace. Love is God.

A lot of times, we find fault in everyone else when the fault is really in us. We have to begin searching for ourselves to see our own shortcomings. When we begin to find this fault in ourselves, it will begin to open the healing process for us with others. A lot of us are hurt over things we thought someone said or done to us. We don't know the truth, and they don't know what they supposedly had done or said. So now, we have you disliking them, and they are being disliked for something they do not understand and are unaware of what they have done or said to you that was offensive. The hatred goes on and on and on and on. This is the way the enemy gets the glory. Because #1, he is the culprit that planted the seed and stirred the pot. The song says, "It's Me, It's Me Oh Lord, Standing in the Need of Prayer," "It's Not My Mother, Not My Father, But It's Me Oh Lord, Standing in the Need of Prayer." How many times have we blamed others for our own downfalls? Instead of accepting the fact that maybe it was me and not them. A lot of us should be further along in our lives but we are being tossed and turned by the enemy, by the troubles of this world and by our own deceitful mind and we are blaming others. It's time to get on board and realize just maybe the enemy is not your neighbor and maybe it is you. We stand in the way of our own breakthrough and deliverance. This is especially when we hold on to hatred and hurt, pain that destroys our joy and uproots our peace.

Mary Clark Norris

Chapter Three

Come unto me, all ye that labour and are heavy laden, and I will give you rest. [29] Take my yoke upon you, and learn of me; for I am meek and lowly in heart: and ye shall find rest unto your souls. [30] For my yoke is easy, and my burden is light.

St. Matthew 11:28-30 (KJV)

Living On His Promises:

IT IS FUNNY how you can trust God for others but not for yourself. Sometimes, we as Christians struggle in our faith and our walk with God. It is only a few of us true born again, bible-reading believers who could admit that out loud. Some of you believe in shouting and speaking in tongues over all of your shortcomings and hang-ups. Unlike myself, I believe in total deliverance and becoming free of the encumbrances that the enemy tries to hold over my head and paralyze me. I know at the end of the day; my struggle is real, but God is too. He said that his yoke is easy, and his burden is light. So, I have to take him at his word while I continue to trust in him and live on his promises. What is the purpose of serving God but not believing in His Promises? You see a true believer understands that deliverance begins at admittance. Once you are able to realize that there is a problem and then announce your struggle out loud, that takes away power from the enemy to hold against you.

19

The enemy then has no channel or outlet to expose you and manipulate the discomfort and agony you may already be facing. It is your faith that completes you and makes you whole. Without your faith, the bible says it is impossible to please God. You are in no condition to satisfy God and bring him favor when you lack in your own faith. You are not in a place to bring deliverance and help others until you line up with the Word of God in your faith and walk with God. The Bible says in Hebrews Chapter 11 that faith is the substance of things hoped for, the evidence of things that are not seen. So, it takes faith in order for you to get things moving and completed in your life. It takes faith to see the works of your labor come to fruition. I know that faith is not visible, but it is what you need in order for you to hold on to your promise. Jesus said, "Come unto me, all ye that labour and are heavy laden and I will give you rest." So, let me go and rest.

2 Corinthians 10:3-5 (KJV)

For though we walk in the flesh, we do not war after the flesh: ⁴ (For the weapons of our warfare are not carnal, but mighty through God to the pulling down of strong holds;) ⁵ Casting down imaginations, and every high thing that exalteth itself against the knowledge of God, and bringing into captivity every thought to the obedience of Christ;

Because we know the enemy is a perpetrator and a deceiver, we must put our best foot forward and be on our guard to disarm the enemy's weapon once he plans to strike. He will plan to strike, and we must be armed for the attack. The Bible says the enemy comes to steal, kill and destroy. I believe it is his main intention and purpose to see our downfalls and defy the plans of God. In Ephesians Chapter 6, the Bible tells us to put on the whole Armour of God that we may be able to stand against the wiles of the devil. Every day we are in battle, but the word tells us that we wrestle not against flesh and blood, but against principalities, against powers, against the rulers of the darkness and spiritual wickedness which are in high places. I think it is important for us to know who our enemies are. The Bible warns us to stay alert and be on guard because the enemy desires to sift us like wheat and scatter us among the wolves. For they will come too and in sheep's clothing prowling around as a roaring lion seeking whom he can devour. But stand firm in your faith and be strong in the Lord for he will never leave you nor forsake you. God has a purpose and a plan for our lives, and in order for us to see his glory, we must adhere to his instructions and take up residence with him. Make no mistake! We have to be on the lookout 24/7 because of our high profile of being a Child of God whose been chosen from the beginning.

The original plan of the enemy is to destroy and in knowing this keeps me fully cautious and watchful. Again, the Bible reminds us to always watch and pray. God has already warned us over and over again about the deceit and cunning ways and the overall plans of the enemy. Not knowing your enemy only sets you up to be entangled with the enemy and most likely being stabbed in the back. The enemy targets your faith because he knows once he gets you faithless, then you will become helpless. This allows the enemy to attack you from behind and blind you from his schemes and tactics that he sends to defeat you. We must always sleep with one eye open so that we won't be caught off guard and sleeping when the enemy breaks into our camp. Why? Because the enemy doesn't sleep so, we have to always stay a step or two ahead of him and his lies. I encourage you to press toward the mark of the high calling and not allow the enemy to hinder your walk with God and the plans he has for your life.

The Bible speaks profoundly about faith and the importance of allowing the measure of your faith to diminish doubt. I was talking with a friend the other day who feels their faith has been tampered with due to the act of soliciting doubt from others. I say it is important to know who you spend your time with or like the Bible says labor among you. As the saying goes, *"you lay with dogs, you will get up with fleas."* I repeat again, "know your enemy!" Do you know that you have won half of your battle once you identify who your enemies are? Your biggest battle is to know who is not for you but against you. Often this is the case in so many situations dealing with relationships. We are not aware of the people who do not mean us any good and only want to destroy our names. These are the folks we are hooking up with and spending the majority of our time with because we think they are our friends. But in actuality, they are your enemies. Their plans are to get us baited in and hooked on a net until they are ready to reel us in like a lifeless worm. Guess what? We fall prey every time to their games and the wickedness to lure us in to cause harm.

We have to become wise in our walk with God. It is time for us to examine ourselves to make sure we are in good standings with the Lord. This helps us to stay rooted and grounded when we are able to search within ourselves and not be so judgmental of our brothers and sisters. This means taking inventory of our own lives to ensure that God is pleased with us in every aspect of it. During this time, we may find that we have some downfalls of our own that we were not aware of and that is okay as long as we are willing to seek the necessary guidance. However, it is vital to make sure we take the necessary actions to resolve the problem and get to a healthier place mentally, emotionally and spiritually. Often, we point the finger at others without being attentive to the ones that are pointing right back at you. We cannot assist others in their walk with God until we have first acknowledged and dealt with our own issues that continue to hold us in bondage. Getting proper healing is essential and critical to our lives in terms of helping others.

The enemy has many tools that he uses to cause us to become discouraged and hopeless. One, he manipulates the Word in our mind to deceive and betray us. Two, he robs our faith and steals our joy. Lastly, he misleads people and fills them with doubt and discouragement. Remember, the enemy is a liar and as the Bible puts it, a father of liars. The biggest lie he has ever told is that his way is better than God's way. The enemy's strategy is to convince you and me that God is not the best thing that has ever happened to us. In the Garden of Eden, the enemy persuaded Adam and Eve by convincing them that his ways are better than God's ways. This actually led to Adam and Eve's death in the Garden for eating off the tree that God had forbidden. You must be committed to Jesus and know that his Word is true and there is none like him. I am a believer that I can do all things through Christ which strengthens me because many times I wanted to shift left, but he redirected me and said to shift right.

My focus and attention have been delayed on many occasions, but God did not allow me to get so far off track that I could not return to him. Instead, he guarded me and shielded me from the storms of life that were sent to annihilate me even when I refused to adhere to his truth. I realize that it was only by the Grace of God that I am still here and able to stand in the midst of doubt and uncertainty. For I know that my Redeemer lives, and he lives in me. Out of all the things that I go through in life, I am reminded that God is my refuge and my strength and a very present help in times of trouble. That word alone gives me hope and courage to know that God will never leave me or forsake his promises to take care of me. In Him, I can always depend.

Romans 5: 1-5 (KJV)

Therefore being justified by faith, we have peace with God through our Lord Jesus Christ: [2] By whom also we have access by faith into this grace wherein we stand, and rejoice in hope of the glory of God. [3] And not only so, but we glory in tribulations also: knowing that tribulation worketh patience; [4] And patience, experience; and experience, hope: [5] And hope maketh not ashamed; because the love of God is shed abroad in our hearts by the Holy Ghost which is given unto us.

Who besides me feels like you are living on your promises? I mean, life can be extremely hard at times, and it can be discouraging to an individual to look to the hills from whence cometh your help. I know that the Bible encourages us to do so, but when you are faced with life trauma and situations, you can barely get out of bed most days. Nevertheless, hold up your head and smile as you move throughout the day from one place to another. Life's woes and circumstances can cause one to doubt the hand of God in their lives. It is easier said than done when it comes to putting your faith in action. I know God is real and I trust his plan. It is unforeseen that sometimes gets confusing. But if we think about it, that is exactly what faith is, something we cannot see. I know I am not the only one who walks in this life but sometimes struggles in their faith. Wholeheartedly, I trust God, and I love him to the core of my being, but sometimes my faith gets weak and often tested daily. In this, we must stand strong in the Lord and know that his Word stands true. You will have tribulations, and you will overcome them by being faithful to God and not allowing the troubles of this world snatch you out of his grace. Whatever you do, stand and rejoice in the hope of his glory,

Chapter Four

And the LORD called Samuel again the third time. And he arose and went to Eli, and said, Here am I; for thou didst call me. And Eli perceived that the LORD had called the child. Therefore Eli said unto Samuel, Go, lie down: and it shall be, if he call thee, that thou shalt say, Speak, LORD; for thy servant heareth. So Samuel went and lay down in his place. And the LORD came, and stood, and called as at other times, Samuel, Samuel. Then Samuel answered, Speak; for thy servant heareth.

I Samuel 3:8-10 (KJV)

Speak Lord, Speak to Me

God speaks many times and in many ways. It is important for us to make sure that we are listening to his voice. I have learned to discern the voice of God by listening to my heart. We have to be open to the voice of God whether his voice is soft and mellow or loud and flamboyant. And, that is whether he speaks in a quiet and peaceful place or a loud and unusual setting. We must be always intentionally listening and waiting for God to speak to us. I walk daily in him purposely, and it is almost like I expect to hear from God morning, noon and night. It is that important for me to hear God's voice on a daily basis so that I am able to partake with him and his Word. This reassures me and provides me with so much comfort and peace to be able to hear the voice of our creator, the almighty Savior of the world.

Now, tell me how big is that? My day is not fulfilled unless I am able to have a dialogue with God about his plans and intentions for my life every morning. Our communication with God should be on an all-time high. I am often in awe of his manifestation, signs and wonders that I get to witness on a daily basis both good and bad. The voice of God is exclusive and very unique but quite simple. It is very clear when he speaks and when he wants to get our attention, he will, and that is whether we are open to him or not. In the Bible, Samuel heard the voice of God and learned the importance of being available to him when he called. My desire is to always be open and available for the master's use even when I am pre-occupied with the daily tasks and troubles of this world. My prayers are to stay rooted and grounded in God that when he calls me, I will be able to know it is him and answer the call. A lot of times, we are not positioned to answer the call of God. This is because we are in our own time zone and separating ourselves from the things of God which hinders us from hearing his voice. Get in place and let God re-position your mind to seek his guidance and leadership as we push to our next level in him. So, Speak Lord, Speak to Me.

Hebrews 2:4 (KJV)

God also bearing them witness, both with signs and wonders, and with divers miracles, and gifts of the Holy Ghost, according to his own will?

I remember one-day riding home from work and God had begun to speak to me in a very clear and directive form. It was no way that I could even confuse myself with the voice of God and what he was saying to me at the time. His message was clear and very concise and unapologetic, I would say. The message from God was to go to a shoe store and help a family.

Now, the fleshy part of me told me that was crazy and especially after I had just left that same store less than an hour past. But the spiritual part of me reminded me that God is not carnal but spiritual and that I needed to listen and adhere to his command. That day many things played a big part in my actions. I know who God is and have heard him speak to me very often but why was this day any different, right? Well, for one, it was no different. However, I allowed my emotions and temperament to get the best of me for a moment. I was tired and had worked all day, not to mention I had just driven 2 hours to get to my destination for the weekend.

So, just like most of us, I hesitated and pondered on my decision over and over again to make my way to the shoe store that evening. And when I thought I had made a conscious decision to go to the shoe store, I turned around and convinced myself that the voice that I heard was not God. So, I turned back around again and proceeded to my destination. As I continued to drive, in the quiet but loud background noise, I could hear God saying to me, *"Didn't I tell you to go to that shoe store!"* Immediately, I turned that car around for the third time, doing a U-turn in the middle of the road. Now, I am sure that was not God's intentions for me to do a U-turn in the middle of the road, but I did. His summon that time, went all through me and brought about so much fear inside of me. I knew that I had heard God speak and his voice was very clear and concise, somewhat like he spoke to Adam and Eve in the garden.

Genesis 3:8 (KJV)

And they heard the voice of the LORD God walking in the garden in the cool of the day: and Adam and his wife hid themselves from the presence of the LORD God amongst the

trees of the garden. And the LORD God called unto Adam, and said unto him, Where art thou?

As I drove in the parking lot, I sat in the car looking from the outside trying to size up who could possibly be inside that God wanted me to help? I tried convincing myself that there were hardly any people in the store and maybe I could just go on to my destination as planned. But I could still feel that sense of fear and of course, guilt on the inside of me telling me to go on ahead and follow the orders that God had given me. So, I prayed a short but earnest prayer before getting out of the car. My prayer was that the person behind the counter in the shoe store would not think that I was some *crazy* lady. Remember, it had only been an hour since I left this same shoe store. I did not know how or what the store clerk would think of me returning and saying what I was about to say to her.

So, I hurriedly walked in the shoe store, before I could hear those voices in my head telling me not to enter. As I proceeded inside, I thought I would walk in the back on the aisle that I had remained earlier and pretend to be looking for something on the floor. Well, that was not working so I went back to the front counter and asked the clerk could I speak with her for a moment? As I approached the counter, there was a family of 4 standing away from the counter as if they were waiting for the clerk's assistance. But the parent motioned her hand for me to go ahead of her and then said that she was waiting on something.

I started to tell the clerk my reasons for re-entering the store after my departure less than an hour ago. I boldly and with conviction in my voice, spoke to her and said that I was commanded by God to come back to the shoe store because there was a family that God wanted me to help financially. The clerk grabbed my hand and turned around and said to the family that she would be right back in a moment. She walked me in the back of the store gripping my hands tightly with sweaty palms. With tears in her eyes, she said to me *"Could you repeat what you just said to me, again."* I then told her that I came to help somebody who God had commanded me to return to the store to help. The store clerk seemed to have a moment of peace of her own by walking back and forth with tears in her eyes saying quietly but out loud *"God if I never knew before who you are, I know today."* The clerk again grabbed my hands and explained that the family of 4 that stood up front was trying to buy some shoes, but they didn't have enough monies. I believe the mother decided after learning that she did not have enough monies to buy her 3 kids' shoes, that she would only buy her oldest son a pair to start school on the following Monday. However, the shoes that the son picked was too much, and she didn't have enough money. After I heard the story concerning the family of 4, immediately I knew this was the family God had sent me to help.

Psalms 27: 5-6 (KJV)

For in the time of trouble he shall hide me in his pavilion: in the secret of his tabernacle shall he hide me; he shall set me up upon a rock. And now shall mine head be lifted up above mine enemies round about me: therefore will I offer in his tabernacle sacrifices of joy; I will sing, yea, I will sing praises unto the LORD.

I walked up to the family and introduced myself. I told them that I was on an assignment by God who had directed me back to the shoe store to help someone. I looked at the mother who had tears in her eyes, and I said that I was sent by God to help her and her family. The mother began to cry and said to me that she had never received such kindness and could not believe that God would send somebody to see about her and her family. I asked that they go and pick out the shoes for her whole family and I would pay for anything else in the store the children would need for school. The mother could not believe what I was saying and asked again, was I sure. Again, I repeated what I spoke earlier. The kids begin to pick out their shoes and other items they wanted and then brought to the counter. I could tell the store clerk could not believe what had happened. She begins to ring up the items with tears in her eyes and saying how unbelievable this act of kindness was and that she had never witnessed such kindness. Afterward, the mother and her 3 children all thanked me and gave me a tight and long hug. One of the children asked if I would take a picture with them so they would remember me. The store clerk then asked for a picture as well with me because she stated that she would report this act of kindness to the general manager, but she was sure they would have a hard time believing that it happened in their store. As I proceeded out the door, the store clerk thanked me. She also said that she had the opportunity to witness God as she has never seen him before. I walked out of that store that day with so many types of feelings and different emotions that were almost overwhelming for me. Tears begin to fall down my face as I tried to put into words why I was chosen that day for such an assignment. All of a sudden, a load of weight disappeared, and I felt freedom again. Oh, how I love my freedom in Jesus.

As I sat there in my car, witnessing the dark of the night, I was amazed at how God had shown up again and discharged his power in such a way to impact his people. The feeling of bringing out a change in someone else's life is so pure and fulfilling. And to think, I was a part of that life-changing occurrence which was powerful and uplifting all at the same time. I am so blessed.

Acts 1: 7-8 (KJV)

And he said unto them, It is not for you to know the times or the seasons, which the Father hath put in his own power. But ye shall receive power, after that the Holy Ghost is come upon you: and ye shall be witnesses unto me both in Jerusalem, and in all Judaea, and in Samaria, and unto the uttermost part of the earth.

As I sit here on my couch and ponder on that day, tears again fill my eyes. It reminds me of how I could have missed the move of God that day when I hesitated to move beyond my fears. In Romans 12:11, the Word tells us not to be slothful in business; fervent in spirit, serving the Lord. How many times has the enemy played into your emotions and convinced you time after time that you are not hearing from God? How many times have you missed the move of God because of being slothful and sluggish about his commandments? Well, I came close to missing the move of God that day, but God pushed me through it. I could have missed God, and that would not have been a good thing. I mean seriously, it is important to discern God and his next move in your life. The enemy is waiting and lurking to see whom he can snatch up and cunningly take their anointing. The reason the anointing is desired so much by that envious enemy is to stop the next God-move in your life. See, the enemy realizes that your next move is going to be your best move. Your next move is going to shake up the camp and pull you out of some stuff that was intended to take you out. **BUT then GOD saw Purpose, and God blocked it!** It does not matter how it looks to the public because what the enemy meant for bad, God is about to turn it around for your good. I am convinced because I stand on

31

the Word of God that there are no weapons that are formed against you shall ever prosper. By the way, if they form, they still won't work. Now, somebody needs to run and tell that!

Chapter Five

One thing have I desired of the LORD, that will I seek after; that I may dwell in the house of the LORD all the days of my life, to behold the beauty of the LORD, and to enquire in his temple. For in the time of trouble he shall hide me in his pavilion: in the secret of his tabernacle shall he hide me; he shall set me up upon a rock.

Psalms 27:4-5 (KJV)

Finding Hope in the Midst of Calamity

Have you heard the Good News? Jesus is Alive and Well! That alone gives me hope and encourages me that God is here with me and will never leave me or forsake me. God is speaking to so many of us today to align our minds with the truth and his Word. I am often amazed by the works that God does to push us to our next level. His word states that we should trust in him with all of our hearts and not lean on our own understanding. However, we oftentimes find ourselves trusting in our own desires and plans instead of trusting in the Lord. We seek so much guidance and direction from the world, and this has been very damaging in the body of Christ. Our minds are distorted by the many lies and deceptions of the enemy. That is why Philippians 2:5 says: Let this mind be in you which was also in Christ Jesus. Christ knew that we would be easily persuaded in our walk and that we would need to be redirected and repositioned during the process. God has uploaded favor to guide us and encourage us as we move forward in aligning ourselves with the truth. I am forever grateful for his compassion and love that keeps me even when I get weary and run in the wrong direction and ignore his instructions for my life.

During our walk, we have lost our hope to trust in God for one more day. We second guess his plans for our life because we do not totally trust him. Man can change his mind with us 99 times and give us 99 excuses, and we will trust man over and over again. However, God has given us 66 books of how to trust him and his plans for our lives, and we question his ability to come through for us every time. God has never once changed or come up short with us, but we continue to not trust him completely with our lives. Believers are the very people who question the plans of God and steer from the truth and his Word just to fit our own desires and longings. I mean, unbelievers do too, but it is the believers, in my opinion, who walk very heavily in unbelief most of the time. We have to get back to the basics. God is God, and he does not change. His Word is the truth, and it gives us life, but we are not in tune with the spirit of God. I am saddened by my lack of trust for him when times get hard, and my life gets out of control. My ability to comprehend his Grace and Mercy can be random and very unpredictable sometimes. However, I only seek to be like him and to get in alignment with the Word of God.

Isaiah 55:6-7 (KJV)

[6] Seek ye the LORD while he may be found, call ye upon him while he is near: [7] Let the wicked forsake his way, and the unrighteous man his thoughts: and let him return unto the

LORD, and he will have mercy upon him; and to our God, for he will abundantly pardon. For my thoughts are not your thoughts, neither are your ways my ways, saith the LORD. [9] For as the heavens are higher than the earth, so are my ways higher than your ways, and my thoughts than your thoughts. [10] For as the rain cometh down, and the snow from heaven, and returneth not thither, but watereth the earth, and maketh it bring forth and bud, that it may give seed to the sower, and bread to the eater: [11] So shall my word be that goeth forth out of my mouth: it shall not return unto me void, but it shall accomplish that which I please, and it shall prosper in the thing whereto I sent it.

Today, God is giving us the one thing that we lack in our walk that will bring us even closer to him, and that is faith. This is the one thing that we cannot see, and we lack in the most. Although, we don't know the plans of God, we continue to trust that our thoughts are not his thoughts and our ways are not his ways. God is bigger than any problem we can even face. The Bible says, faith is the substance of things hoped for, but the evidence of things not seen. Although, we cannot see the hands of God and the entire outlet to his blessings we must believe that his Word shall not return unto him void. With God, A promise is a promise. He is extending us with hope that will bring about the peace that surpasses all understandings in him. You no longer have to look to man for answers, but we can look to the hills from which cometh all of our help knowing all of our help comes from the Lord. We no longer must lean on our own understanding and our ways of doing things, but we can put our trust in the Lord and know that he will give us the desires of our heart in the midst of chaos. The enemy meant it for bad, but God meant it for your good. I know it doesn't seem like it is going to work out for your good. I know that it may get worse before it gets better. I know that it may seem like the whole world is against you and they may be, but that is not your problem. God is the strongest power and because he is you are not defeated. You must stay focused and hold on to your faith and know that God did not bring you this far to leave you. In times like these, you must stand still and wait on the Lord so that one day you will be able to see the fruits of your labor. Your long nights of waiting were not in vain. Your tears have not been wasted. Your hard work has not been overlooked. Just know that your reward is right around the corner and it is packaged just for you signed, sealed and delivered.

Many times, we can be waiting on an arrival of a package one way, and God decides to deliver it another. This is how God works. His plan is not like ours. His thoughts are above our thoughts. We cannot try to box God in and expect him to do things our way. God is in charge of our lives, and he only wants what is best for us. However, we must be humble and learn to trust his plan. We must recognize God and his greater works because he is the author and the finisher of our faith. Therefore, it is not over until God says that it is over. He has the master plan and is able to unlock any door that has been locked by the enemy. We have to remember, God wants us to trust him even when it does not look promising and hopeful. Although, the doctors may walk away from your bed and say the worst scenario about your situation, you must believe that the trying of your faith still works patience. God has a plan for your life. You must believe by His stripes, you are healed. You must believe that you are the head and not the tail, above and not beneath. Everything that God has promised you in his Word is the truth, the whole truth and nothing but the truth, so help me God.

Jeremiah 29:11 (KJV)

For I know the thoughts that I think toward you, saith the LORD, thoughts of peace, and not of evil, to give you an expected end.

God has already made up his mind about you. He loves you and only wants what is best for your life. I know the enemy tells you something totally different, but that is deception baby and don't buy it. You must not give in to the temptation of the enemy. You are already victorious, and the enemy knows it. That is why he continues to go after the gifts that are planted on the inside of you. Fight him for your gifts and fight him for your life. You must remember, he is the opponent and he never fights fair that is why the Bible tells us that the enemy comes to steal, kill and destroy. So, suit up and get in gear because this time it is about to be on. Don't just sit there and let the enemy come into your house, demand your stuff, and then get them and leave. Well, you may leave, but it won't be without this fight. It is time to stand up for what is right and fight for your family. If ever, I am going down in a battle, it will not be because I did not fight. We must remember when we are up against the enemy; we cannot fear but keep our faith and know God is with us always. I think David can understand me when I say; sometimes our problems can look bigger than the problem solver. But we must stay the course and don't lose our faith in God and what he can do in any situation that we may encounter. David's plan to destroy Goliath worked because he remembered that God was with him and promised to never leave him even in the midst of chaos. It was not David's strength that defeated the giant. It was David's faith. The Bible says in I John 5:4 For whatsoever is born of God overcometh the world: and this is the victory that overcometh the world, even our faith. I am a believer and an overcomer, and I declare Victory over any obstacle or hurdle that I face and you must too.

I can stand to lose when I know I have tried to win and fought a good fight. What gets me is when people allow the enemy to bombard their homes and destroy their children and not put up a fight. I am not talking about putting your hands on anyone, but what I am talking about is using your weapons to fight the enemy by going into his camp and declaring war. It is time to take back your children, grandchildren, spouse, neighbor, neighbor's neighbor and your church and the list goes on. We must DECLARE, and DECREE VICTORY is MINE! You must know prayer is your weapon. The Word of God is also your weapon; we must use them and begin to see God fight for us in every aspect of our lives.

Ephesians 6:11-13 (KJV)

Put on the whole armour of God, that ye may be able to stand against the wiles of the devil. For we wrestle not against flesh and blood, but against principalities, against powers, against the rulers of the darkness of this world, against spiritual wickedness in high places. Wherefore take unto you the whole armour of God, that ye may be able to withstand in the evil day, and having done all, to stand.

I hate to be the bearer of bad news for you and your entire family, but the enemy does not like you. He doesn't like your mama, daddy, sister, brother, nieces, nephews, your children, and your cousins, just to be clear. And if you have some little ones running around, he doesn't like them either. The enemy's plan is to take you out by force. Once, you truly understand that then and only then will you understand that he is not your friend but a trickster. His desire is to drag you by your hair and your coat tale in some dry and lonely place so that he could devour you and make you consider suicide. Now, that you know who he is and what he is capable of doing, get rid of him and all of his junk. Some of you continue to share ties with the enemy, and that is why he constantly tortures your mind. Then you wonder why your mind is always filled with negative thoughts and negative actions follows is because you have not been delivered from the snare of the fowler. You are still dipping in the pool where Satan resides and accepting his proposals whenever he shows up. You are still lying, cursing, fornicating, bite biting and some of the other 12 commandments that God has forbidden. It is time to break ties of the enemy and declare and decree in the atmosphere that you are no longer bound but free and free indeed. We fight not against flesh and blood but against Satan who is trying to manipulate our minds and sentence us to life for our mistakes and shortcomings of our past. But God said if I confess my sins that he is faithful and just to forgive us our sins and to cleanse us from all unrighteousness. Know your enemy and his tactics so that you will not be deceived in this walk. Every step you take should be taken by faith in the Name of the Father, Son, and the Holy Ghost. The Trinity.

St. Matthew 11:12 (KJV)

And from the days of John the Baptist until now the kingdom of heaven suffereth violence, and the violent take it by force.

Chapter Six

Now Faith is the substance of things hoped for, the evidence of things not
seen.

Hebrews 11: 1 (KJV)

Trust the Process

In order to reach our destiny and purpose, we must get up and walk.
Oftentimes, it is not about how we fell but how we get back up. In doing
that we must be willing to trust the process. I am a believer that faith is that
PUSH that you normally don't see but can feel when you are about to
throw in the towel. We all have experienced that push at some point of time
in our lives. That is whether we can admit that or not. The other day, I was
sharing thoughts with a special friend of mine about the importance of
staying focused as you walk in God's purpose. Sometimes it is not about
the way things look or even what people may think about you. It is about
walking in the will of God and being faithful in your walk. Sometimes the
billows may roll, and even the storm clouds may rise in our lives, but we
must be determined to *succeed* at all cost by staying rooted and grounded in
the Word of God. This goes back to trusting the process. I am not
insinuating that it will be easy as 1,2,3 or ABC but what I am saying is that it
will be worth every step. When we totally surrender our will to God, he

purposely takes charge over our lives and begins to lead the way. By the way, I am a living witness that it is not easy getting up every day and motivating yourself to push beyond the limits of your past. Especially, when you feel like you are in this thing called *"life"* alone. Life can be brutal and very challenging as it is and adding anything else to the mix is like making a strong concoction that was mixed with lemonade and grapefruit juice. But what I have learned is that this is where faith must be incorporated. It is by faith that our circumstances will change and take a turnaround for the better. It is our faith that brings us to the problem and allows us to face it head on and not face a collision. Most of the time that is not knowing what is ahead and possible the outcome but trusting that God will take care of you through every valley or mountain you will have to climb.

Some of the things in my life right now that I am facing, don't look promising but I know I have to hang on to God's unchanging hands and trust that he will see me through. So, I will continue to wake up every day and smile even when I feel like crying. I realize that faith is not about what I can see in front of me but what I cannot see. And I can see God turning some things around in my life and in my favor. I have nothing but faith to believe God as I commit myself to him and his Word. I am going to trust that God will allow these tests to become my testimony and it all works out for my good. Like Job, I will wait until my change comes and so shall I see the salvation of the Lord.

A lot of time, the challenges we face in life is not about us, but about God trying to use us to help somebody else get a breakthrough. I know that can be difficult for you and me to understand. My prayers during these tough times in my life are that I don't miss the true message from God but that I bring him glory through my attitude as I continue to press through the mark. In this walk of life, I am truly learning more and more on how to have the patience for things and people that I had ever imagined. Today, I think I realize more than ever that the trying of my faith worketh patience. Seriously, be careful when you ask God for patience. It will cost you a great deal. I took it lightly when I used to hear people say that and now, I believe that fully. You just never know the route God will take as he begins to instill patience in you. Again, I must warn you, there will be a price to pay. But, it will all work out for your good. All you have to do is trust the process.

Psalms 18:1-3 (KJV)

I will love thee, O LORD, my strength. The LORD is my rock, and my fortress, and my deliverer; my God, my strength, in whom I will trust; my buckler, and the horn of my salvation, and my high tower. I will call upon the LORD, who is worthy to be praised: so shall I be saved from mine enemies.

If there is one thing that I know and have learned through the reading of the book of Job and that is "true patience" suffers long. I could never compare nor, would I want to compare the setbacks that I have experienced in my lifetime to this great man of God that we call, Job. Definitely, he was a force to be reckoned with. He was powerful in his acts. He was very strong and courageous. He is the epitome of "strength." Job was a warrior, a mighty man of valor. He knew the importance of trusting God fully in spite of what it looked like to his friends and his wife. Job loved God, and God loved Job. God knew the strength of Job, and he blessed Job for his faithfulness.

Job had the courage and strength to endure even when he lost everything, and still, he refused to curse God and die. You just don't get that kind of faith or patience overnight. I believe the patience Job had was created on the cross when Jesus was crucified. I mean the Bible says Job suffered greatly and lost everything he owned and even lost all of his children. Now, for me, that is where fasting and praying would be my guide. The thought of losing a child is disturbing enough just to think about it. But, losing all of your children, I believe can be devastating and right out heart-wrenching.

A special friend of mine, Tonya Morris and her husband, Charles Morris knows these feelings all too well. They have experienced losing not one child but their *only* two children and within short of 6 months apart. I cannot even imagine the hurt and pain that comes with this kind of loss. And it breaks my heart to even think about it. I have watched, comforted, consoled and supported my friend, Tonya and her husband through both of their losses and not one time have I witnessed them reject and/or deny who God is and the strength of his power. Their faith in God has been consistent and reputable through all of the turmoil and devastation they have experienced. They have proven that the strength of God lives down on the inside of them. It is through the Almighty God and the power of his might that she and her husband continue to build relationships and be empowered even in the midst of chaos and confusion. I have watched my friend, Tonya in the midst of her suffering encourage other family and friends to push through their trials as she battled her own. I have held her hand as she cried numerous times as we sat just to commune in fellowship with one another. I have watched her tears flow many times as it was nothing, I could do but hold her hands and comfort her through her pain. On occasions, I would sing to her to help wash the pain away. She would laugh and often cry through it all but not one time has she ever doubted God and the power he holds in his hands. Now, if that is not a sign of a true warrior, then I do not know one. It is without fail, God is their refuge and their strength in times of trouble, and they continue to represent him well.

As I reflect, I remember after a very short period of time after burying their sons (both occasions); I witnessed Tonya and her husband, Charles back in church on that Sunday morning dancing and praising God. As I watched them, it helped to increase the faith in me. They were there sitting on the pews listening to our pastor as he preached. I was able to see God not only in their words but in their actions as well. I thought to myself, if they can trust God to this magnitude during this type of loss, then there is nothing that will be able to STOP their flow. At that moment, it dawned on me that my friend was dancing on broken bones.

Now, had I not witnessed this type of faith and act of strength, it may have been difficult for me to believe. The strength and faith in God that they have is immense. My own faith has kicked up a notch as I continue to watch them live their life out loud as they walk in silence enduring the pain. In spite of their daily routines, they continue to push through the storms of life looking to family and friends for support and lasting memories as they try to rebuild their lives on broken bones. I can only imagine the type of strength they will have as they continue to trust the process and walk by faith and not by sight. Now, that demonstrates not only the measure of their strength in this walk but their assurance in God as they continue to build their hope on things eternal. When we trust God and not our own intellect, God will step in and do the imaginable. When you no longer rely on your own strength to get through your trials and tribulations, but the strength of God then you have found the ingredients to **FAITH**.

Proverbs 3:5-6 (KJV)

Trust in the Lord with all thine heart; and lean not unto thine own understanding. In all thy ways acknowledge him, and he shall direct thy paths.

Trusting the process is the evidence of things not seen. Faith is not visual. You cannot see faith. You just have to trust and believe the process and know that it is going to work for your good and in your favor. Now, that is double for your trouble. God has not given us the spirit of fear, but he has given us the level of faith to move beyond our own desires and expectations. You have to know that we are already winners in the Kingdom of God. I believe no matter what, it's my winning season. I have lost so many times in the past to the point that it is not funny. I have lost cars, houses, clothes, jobs, pets, and loved ones. But I refuse to lose anything else. It is time to trust the process. Stepping out of your comfort zone and trust God beyond what you can feel or what you can see. I know it can be tough and alarming at times, but I refuse to give in or give up due to the many of adversities I have experienced along the way. I am not built to break. I am a daughter of the King, the Most-High God.

I have learned earlier on by trial and error that there will be tests and trials that I will face that will try to push me to the edge of giving up. Now, that I know this, I know that I have to be strong and courageous in this battle. I am determined to press to my promise and not be focused on what it looks like on the other side of nowhere. An orange can sometimes look like grapefruit to me, but I know they are not the same, and neither tastes the same. What I am trying to say, I cannot allow what my life looks like to you right now determine the outcome of my future. If it is to be, it is up to me to make it happen for me. I want to encourage you, my reader, to live life to the fullest. Dance like nobody is watching. Sing as nobody is listening (maybe low if you cannot hold a note). Just live and know that you are a seed that has been planted on the good ground. As you wait on growth and maturity, allow God to water you and preserve you for your due season. For you are standing on Holy ground.

Psalms 28:7-8 (KJV)

The Lord is my strength and my shield; my heart trusted in him, and I am helped: therefore my heart greatly rejoiceth; and with my song will I praise him. The Lord is my strength, and he is the saving strength of his anointed.

The Lord is my strength no matter what it looks or how I may feel on the inside. My full trust is in the Lord and the power of his might. We must believe that the work has already begun in us; my prayer is that God will prune us as he continues to finish what he has started within us. Philippians 1: 6 reminds me of this daily to be confident of this very thing, that he which hath begun a good work in you will perform it until the day of Jesus Christ. I have to believe that God has already written the end of my story. I know that sometimes people can try to close the book on you without the final say from God. People do not understand the fact of letting go of your past. They will continue going back visiting your past and how you use to live, what you use to do and how you use to treat others. Well, I have learned that you have to be transparent with people from the beginning of any conversation about discussing you and your past. First, I am not that person anymore. Simply, don't entertain it. Make it crystal clear that any discussion about you and your past is off limits. You have to be careful. People are deceitful and they will try to discuss your past to hide their present shenanigans. Is it not like the enemy? Trying to take you down a path that God has delivered you from. Don't go and don't allow anyone to have the pleasure of taking you back. Oftentimes, people can *"forget"* the pile of dirt that is stacked so high on the side of their own house but see your dirt coming through the gate. *I think we all need to read St. Matthew 7:3-5 and then repent and get the mote out of their own eye before trying to find the beam in thy brother's eye.*

I count it all joy when I am tested and tried by the fire. For then I know it is not about me but my purpose. The enemy desire is to steal my destiny. You have to stay focused in your walk with God and not allow the commotion and noise of the enemy to convince you to heed to his persuasion. The Bible reminds us not to let nothing separate us from the love of God. We have to be fully committed to the will of God and his love for us. God encourages us to trust only in him and his plans for our lives, and I want to encourage you in scripture found in I Corinthians to be steadfast, unmovable, always abounding in the work of the Lord knowing that your labour is not in vain in the Lord. The plan of the enemy is to take away your joy, terminate your peace and destroy your praise. If you allow him to have access to your life in any way, he will do just that and much more. Remember, he comes to drive, no more riding with the devil. Through all of this, I pray that your faith will not fail in the Lord. God is your strength.

James 1: 2-3 (KJV)

My brethren, count it all joy when ye fall into divers temptations; knowing this, that the trying of your faith worketh patience.

We all have experienced our fair share of struggles, and sometimes we go through hardships and turmoil which can be very frustrating. I have experienced those moments not long ago. I was fed up with the enemy coming after my family. A girl could only take so much. You know how it is when you mess around with somebody's family. I felt like that little girl again in 2nd grade at Southside Elementary School when that little boy talked about my mama. You know how it was when you were little, and someone talked about your mama. I never could understand why that word *"your mama"* had a substantial impact on me. It brought out tears for me quickly. I didn't know how to fight so I would just cry when someone talked about my mama. I guess it's the "disrespect" factor behind it. I don't know. I just know when it comes to family and disrespecting family members you have to know that you are walking a thin line between love and hate. This frustrates me when those types of things happen because I know that the enemy takes pleasure out of those kind of behaviors. I was ready to go into the enemy's camp and fight back and reclaim my family's time or better yet, family tree. However, I was able to do that through prayer and fasting. We were being tried by the fire one thing after another. But I was determined to press forward, and I refused to quit praying and seeking God for a breakthrough. You have to remember, the enemy does not like families and does not want families to be united. The aim is to kill, steal and destroy. Well, I got news for him: No Weapon Formed Against Me and Mines Shall Prosper!

Romans 12:17-21 (KJV)

Recompense to no man evil for evil. Provide things honest in the sight of all men. If it be possible, as much as lieth in you, live peaceably with all men. Dearly beloved, avenge not yourselves, but rather give place unto wrath: for it is written, Vengeance is mine; I will repay, saith the Lord. Therefore if

thine enemy hunger, feed him; if he thirst, give him drink: for in so doing thou shalt heap coals of fire on his head. Be not overcome of evil, but overcome evil with good.

Chapter Seven

For this thing I besought the Lord thrice, that it might depart from me.
And he said unto me, My grace is sufficient for thee: for my strength is
made perfect in weakness. Most gladly therefore will I rather glory in my
infirmities, that the power of Christ may rest upon me.

II Corinthians 12: 8-9 (KJV)

Grace and Deliverance

We live every day only but by the grace of God. We do not know our
next move. I know that sometimes, we think that we do, but we don't. It is
only by the Grace of God that we live, and move, and have our being. It is
God who provides, and it is he who delivers on every Word. We are far
from deserving anything. It is God who gives us the grace that we do not
deserve. Some people often confuse grace and karma. Well, grace is the
opposite of karma. I hear people often say *"karma"* is what you will get
because it is what you deserve. But I thank God that he is not petty like us.
He gives us grace although he knows we have done nothing to deserve it,
but he gives it to us anyway. Now, that is love and the love of a father. I can
recall many occasions that I have sinned against God and right during my
mess that I created, God's grace protected me anyway. This is what real
grace looks like. It is clearly the beauty of his strength that covers me and
shields me even in my weakness.

2 Timothy 1:9 (KJV)

Who hath saved us, and called us with an holy calling, not according to our works, but according to his own purpose and grace, which was given us in Christ Jesus before the world began,

In every aspect of my life, God's grace is sufficient. I have heard this scripture read in the Bible so many times. However, it was that very moment that brought me to my knees to really the meaning of grace. I had tried everything to soothe the pain, but nothing worked. I was tired but mainly fed up with life's ups and downs. Relationships were hard and very complicated at the time. I was too young to even understand it all anyway. Just like many other young women who step into what we call "grown folk stuff" before your time. You know how it is. We think we have grown before we get grown. We have a desire to do "grown folks' stuff" but have no sense of direction and idea of the "grown folks' stuff." To be honest with you, I was in a battle with myself. I suffered from self-love and self-actualization. I just never felt I was ever good enough. Because I was already undergoing a battle in my relationship, I became even more bitter and broken on the inside. I needed help but was afraid to let anyone know that I needed it. So, I hid myself from the outside world by painting my face with a smile and laughs that would bring attention to myself but would hide all my insecurities. I stayed around people because I did not want any of my family and friends to see my silent woes.

So, I figured my presence would hide all of my pain and sorrow. It did for a while, I thought. I was just too miserable living and hiding behind a mask parading back and forth with an empty cup. God Forbid. I wanted to end everything, my life and the pain that came with it. It was God who showed up in the midst of my turmoil and pain and graced me that dreadful day and said, "I will never leave you, nor forsake you." He then whispered in my ear again and said, "TAKE MY YOKE UPON YOU AND LEARN OF ME, FOR MY YOKE IS EASY, AND MY BURDEN IS LIGHT." From that day, I have held on to God's hands, and I shall never let go because I know, he's got me. So, I want to encourage you today that not only is he holding my hand, but he is holding yours too. God is saying to you to trust in his plans for your life. I don't care what it looks like or how bad you think it may be. God's got you! So, what if you may have done the unthinkable, God still has you covered. His Word tells me that his LOVE never fails. So, pick yourself up, brush yourself off and wipe your pretty eyes, and get busy living your best life because God's got you.

Psalms 24:7-8 (KJV)

Lift up your heads, O ye gates; and be ye lift up, ye everlasting doors; and the King of glory shall come in. Who is this King of glory? The LORD strong and mighty, the LORD mighty in battle.

Like many of you, I have dishonored God on so many levels and failed to keep my promises to him. I am ashamed of the countless times, I have disappointed him by not trusting in his will as I doubted his plans over my life. Sometimes, when life shows up, it can be hard to continue to trust God's plan for your family and especially when it is looking dim and gloomy. As a believer, I do know who God is. But even in my walk, discouragement and doubt seem to creep in and interrupts my peace. That is why we must stay in the face of God and seek him for guidance, leadership, and clarity. It is he who guides me into all truth. It is time to prepare and armor up in our gear and get ready for battle. The enemy will come in like a flood, but my God says he shall lift up a standard against him. I want to encourage you as I encourage myself as well; look to the hills from whence cometh all our help for it cometh from the Lord, which made heaven and earth. The Bible also says, He will not suffer thou foot to be moved: he that keepeth thee will not slumber nor sleep. This scripture assures me that God is always near and I can lean on him no matter what the outcome may look like because he will never leave me nor forsake me. That is his promise, and I take him at his Word. I want to say Thank you God for loving me in spite of all my shortcomings along with my ranting and raving sometimes. God is love and his mercy endureth unto all generations. His love for me is without measure, and I am grateful to be called a daughter of the King. I approve of this message.

Ephesians 6:11 (KJV)

Put on the whole armour of God, that ye may be able to stand against the wiles of the devil.

I am so thankful to God for his forgiveness and the many times he has delivered me from bondage, other people's expectations, and fear. These are the things that can keep us bound and lost in despair. God wants us to be free from those strongholds and the bondage of man. There are times where we will have to not take down but stand against the enemy's plans to defeat us. We have to declare victory in our fight. I am who I am today because God is who he is in my life right now. It is only by his grace that he continues to keep me solid and stable. Grace is that unwavering, yet undeserved, and unmerited favor of God that we are in need of daily. The grace of God has breathed life back into me so many times and on so many occasions. I could never repay God for all he has done for me even if I tried. So many times, I have failed God because of my disobedience and arrogance because I wanted to do things my way and in my own timing. I did not realize without God that I was not only helpless but hopeless as well. Today, I am forever grateful for his everlasting love and his grace that sustained me and helped me in my weakest moments. I am able to stand against the enemy and declare that through it all I have learned to trust in Jesus and I have learned to trust in God.

Titus 2: 9-11 (KJV)

Exhort servants to be obedient unto their own masters, and to please them well in all things; not answering again; Not purloining, but shewing all good fidelity; that they may adorn the doctrine of God our Saviour in all things. For the grace of God that bringeth salvation hath appeared to all men.

Give ear to my prayer, O God, as they walk in your grace and deliverance. My prayer today is not about me but for others. How many times do we say that? Often times, when we pray it is about what God can do for you. How about what you ask God to do for your neighbor next door and the neighbor across the street. We never know what others are going through and some of the burdens they are carrying. We can be so in tune with our own needs and problems that we neglect the people around us. Well, let us move beyond self today and seek God on behalf of others who are suffering in silence. Maybe you can go out of your way to make someone else smile by lending a helping hand and a listening ear.

You will be surprised about how many people you know and talk to on a daily basis that are struggling with suicide and depression. Suicide is the leading cause of death among us. It is time to have the talk and listen to someone who may feel depressed and maybe in despair. A lot of time, a person suffering from depression may look put together and seemingly happy, and this can be misleading. Today, let us ask God to help us and allow the Holy Spirit to lead us so that we can discern what we can do to help and empower others. I don't want another person in my circle to lose their life due to suicide. I pray that God will give us the insight and the discernment we need in order to help someone who is battling depression and feeling hopeless. There is hope in Jesus. I just want to help someone to know this today and know that Jesus loves them no matter what they are going through.

There are days when I feel alone and abandoned. Sometimes, I have to encourage myself to get out of bed and start my day. Oftentimes, I just want to lay there and not deal with people and my problems. I have to remind myself sometimes that the greater is on the inside of me and that I can do all things because Christ said that I have the strength to do so. I become weary and worried about how others perceive me, and the judging factor is off the chart. People will judge you based on what you wear, look and what you drive. This is ridiculous but that is the world we are living in, and it is so sad, to say the least. Another reason we have to put our trust in Jesus and not depend on man but look up unto him and know that he can fix every situation we face.

I know that it is not always easy, and God never said that it would be. So, I know that although life has its ups and downs, I must continue to stay focused on the things of God and not allow the outside world to influence my decisions and my goals moving forward. As I pondered for a moment, I am reminded of the God that I serve and his Word that says, I will never leave you or forsake you. I have to believe that. I know life happens and we are often faced with turmoil and destruction in every corner of our life, but we have to believe, God is our Deliverer. And in him, I will trust.

Hebrews 4: 16 (KJV)

Let us therefore come boldly unto the throne of grace, that we may obtain mercy, and find grace to help in time of need

Chapter Eight

The righteous cry, and the LORD heareth, and delivereth them out of all their troubles. The LORD is nigh unto them that are of a broken heart; and saveth such as be of a contrite spirit. Many are the afflictions of the righteous: but the LORD delivereth him out of them all.

Psalms 34: 17-19 (KJV)

Broken and Bruised

Heartbreak hurts. The experience of heartbreak can be so intense that it can feel like physical pain. If you have never had a broken heart, be thankful. But, let me warn you, it can tear you apart. I was reading in the newspaper last week about a 76-year-old woman who died of a broken heart. She and her spouse were married over 50 years when he passed, and 2 weeks later, doctors said that the woman died of a broken heart. This type of pain can be brutal and vicious. I don't wish this on my worst enemy. It feels like your heart is crumbling into tiny pieces. One thing that I can remember from it all is that love hurts. I can recall that dreadful day that aimed to snatch away my peace of mind. Sometimes, I can still hear the sound of people talking loud in the background as I tried to drown out my thoughts. I can still hear the telephone ringing hot off the line and with the loud echoes in the background. The door slammed opened, and a man in a navy-blue uniform walked over to me and said, "Are you, Mary Norris?" Right before I could answer clearly, he handed me a brown long envelope and said, "Madam, you have been served." My heart dropped, and it began to beat really fast and loud. I thought the entire office could hear it. I believe for a minute or so, and my heart flatlined. It had to because I could no longer hear my heart beating. Then suddenly, the rhythm of my heartbeat started back pounding once again. Afterward, I could feel my heart breaking into many small pieces. It hurt, and for a second, I was numb. My heart was crushed. Something went all through me. For a brief moment, I could not breathe. I thought I was about to have a panic attack. It was like I was gasping for air but could not breathe. I believe I took part in the mannequin challenge for a moment. I just stood there because I could not move. I was screaming for help on the inside, but apparently, nobody could hear me. "Lord why have you forsaken me?" I screamed. For the next 5 to 7 minutes I stood there while my whole life flashed in front of me. How in the world could this be, I thought? Subsequently, I gathered myself and my thoughts and slowly walked away and back to my office with a broken heart and small bits of my pride. On that day, I was introduced to what it means to be broken and bruised.

That day began the many days of feeling hopeless and helpless all wrapped in one package. I have had some good days, and I have had some bad days. Much of my good days have outweighed my bad days though I could not see it at the time. However, most of my bad days have been captioned "I Don't Look like What I've Been Through." I need to make that my slogan and anthem for that year because it almost took me out of here. But God. And I mean that with every breath that I breathe. Only a few people who have been through something can agree with me that the

"But God" interpretation has deep meaning and should not be taken lightly. Anybody cannot use "But God" unless you know that it was nobody but God that blocked the enemy's plan to suffocate you. It is only by the grace of God that has kept me from falling into the miry clay and not getting stuck in my own mess. There have been times that I wanted to turn in my gloves and walk away from the fight. This is especially when I was already both broken and bruised. Yet, every time I begin to walk away from the fight, something deep on the inside of me gave me extra strength and encouraged my heart to keep pumping. That is why I keep pushing and coming back just for a little more of Jesus. More is what I desire of him. More of his glory. More of his anointing. More of his power. Just more of Jesus and his love. My desire is to give God more of me as he continues to give me more of him. I just want to return the favor and honor him.

Every day has not always been Sunday, and I know this. However, through it all, God has given me more joy, peace and love and all in the midst of my pain and my struggles. Even when I was not deserving or worthy of his substances, he never gave up on me. I continue to find peace and harmony in his presence, and that is where I long to be, in his presence. The other day, I heard God speak to me and said, "Tell my people to Face-time me." I quickly took that request for myself and got in the face of Jesus. We need to know that God desires one on one time with us and in his presence. God was speaking and requesting more time with him and less time with everything else that we deem a priority. All God wants from us is our time in worship face to face with him. It is my belief that God wants to set his people free from being bound and confused. Freedom is on the horizon, and it is on the other side of your breakthrough. Now, all we have to do is to get up and go get it. I have made up my mind, despite the attacks and counterattacks upon my life, I will always be team Jesus and have a

"Yes" in my mouth. I am committed to serving God, and I will continue to look to the hills from which cometh all my help for all my help cometh from the Lord. There is no point of turning around now because you are too close to recovery.

Psalms 121 (KJV)

I will lift up mine eyes unto the hills, from whence cometh my help. My help cometh from the LORD, which made heaven and earth. He will not suffer thy foot to be moved: he that keepeth thee will not slumber.

Some of you may have experienced the same type of pain that I once experienced. This pain what I am talking about seems to torment your spirit and chew at your flesh piece by piece. Does the pain ever go away? I don't know but what I do know is that this same pain comes back to haunt me in my sleep sometimes. It comes to remind me of the broken pieces that were once left on the inside of me. That is why it is important to get healed from hurt and being broken. When you have been deeply wounded, the pain tends to linger around and wait on the next victim. That is why the saying goes "Hurt people, hurt people." You have to be careful with this type of hurt because it can be dreadful. Many of you have been broken and bruised and because of the level of pain that you have suffered has caused you to become bitter while broken. Therefore, most of us are not effective in our relationships because those broken pieces of the past have been lying dormant on the inside waiting on the next person to hurt. That is why total healing is so important. Because when the healing process does not take shape after being hurt, it can become drastic and damaging and cause an enormous amount of bitterness and resentment. Remember, the broken pieces that were left on the inside of you are not dead but sleeping and when you are in a new relationship those pieces of the past that have left you almost paralyzed begin to rise back up. Then the cycle continues to go around and around until you begin to seek wholeness and fulfillment as a covering. You will not be able to move forward in a relationship or grow in God until you have totally healed from this complexity of pain. That is why many people are in God's house serving and are bitter and broken. I think, a lot of time, we feel trapped and don't know how to get free from the bondage. So instead, we get comfortable and hide behind positions and titles and hope we are not uncovered and exposed any time soon. Most of us have been raised in the church, and we know how to look and how to act churchy. We know just what to say and how to act when we say it. The drums and the keyboard are the edges that can push us to our next shout. We speak in tongues in the right key and give it a boost with a minor chord. We begin our testimony in the same format "First giving honor to God who is the head of my life," and we end it with the phrase, "Those of you, who know the words of prayer, pray for my strength in the Lord." All while we are broken and bruised. We are shouting, but we are broken. We are singing on the Praise and Worship team, but we are broken. We are preaching, and the whole church is getting blessed, but we are broken. We are selling out arenas all over the world, and people are being saved and delivered, but we are still broken. We are just serving in our brokenness. True healing begins with admittance and repentance. If you desire to be healed, delivered and set free, you have to surrender all to God and allow him to heal the broken pieces in your heart and put you back together again. Today, God wants to heal you where you hurt.

Psalms 147:3 (KJV)

He healeth the broken in heart, and bindeth up their wounds.

Our world is in a place of the unfamiliar. It seems like everything from our home, schools, communities, government and our churches are all in a dark and dreary place. Prayer has been attacked and then abolished from our schools, and our world is in need of healing. There was a time when we could run to the church for safety to get what we needed when times got hard. Now, people are running from the church. I remember growing up as a little girl, and the church was our refuge and our safe place where we would go to gather strength and be happy. The church was always the answer to everything when times were hard for our family. Church to us was like the club to some folks. The closest I ever been to the club, to say the least.

I cannot recall one time in my life where the church was not a part of my life growing up. Church was our grocery store. If we ran out of food, we could always go to the church for help and load up on some can goods out of the church's food pantry. Church was also our financial institution. When money was low, and bills piled up, we could always count on the church to help with paying a light bill or a water bill just to get us over to the next month. Believe it or not, the church also became the beauty salon. If anyone needed a hairdo for church on Sunday morning, we could always count on somebody in the church who was an aspiring Beautician or Barber and style/cut your hair for free.

Those were the good old days. I am so grateful for my parents who drove me to church to every Bible Study, Prayer Meeting, Choir Rehearsal, Church Anniversary and regular Sunday Morning Worship just to make sure that I had a strong and solid foundation. Even though we stayed in church all day, missing breakfast, lunch, and dinner, we were there and looked forward to coming back the next following Sunday. Nevertheless, I am grateful for the upbringing and all the sacrifices that were made to get me where I am today. Looking ahead and directly in front of me, and seeing the danger and viciousness all around me, I could never imagine my life without God in it.

St. Mark 16:17 (KJV)

And these signs shall follow them that believe; In my name shall they cast out devils; they shall speak with new tongues.

I don't know what to make of these times. "What is this world coming to," I wonder? Has church lost its flavor or its Savior? There is no real level of healing, signs, and wonders taking place in the house of God anymore. Why? Could it be that the church has become commercialized and more about the money, prestige, and titles instead of the souls of the people? The Bible said that we should be like him. It is evident in the Bible that God healed the sick and caused the lame to walk again. There were many signs and wonders all around when Jesus himself went out performing miracles in the streets and on every corner. There is a disconnect somewhere. It breaks my heart to see how the churches all around fail to seek God and stay in his face for the evidence of his power on "high to fall" during worship? But, instead, we rush the service because we have an agenda and a program to follow. What about the people who came to church for deliverance and to be set free from soul ties and other strongholds? Do we consider them anymore?

Maybe, I am just too passionate about all of this. We have people that come to the house of God broken and bruised, and we just sit there Sunday after Sunday watching them bleed. So, we sit Sunday after Sunday ladies, with our white suits and big fancy hats and gold or silver high heel shoes waiting for an opportunity to testify just to be seen. While all the time, you have people sitting in the pews and screaming on the inside for help. Of course, you did not discern that the visitor on your left was in pain and crying with tears falling from their eyes throughout the entire service. Well, you probably could not see their pain because you were so busy testifying and making a big deal about your own. Ladies, we have to do better. They tell me when you know better, you do better.

I don't want to be accused of being bias so men, you have to do better also. There you sit in your deacon's corner with your pinstriped black suits with matching socks and matching tie on looking important but mean. During the entire time, you continued to watch the clock every 10 minutes as the pastor continues to preach his heart out about sin and persecution. You missed the topic of the sermon because you were so busy trying to watch what time the pastor started his song so that you can calculate and complain later to the deacon board how long the pastor preached. Never did you notice that the young man in the first pew kept his head down the entire time because he could not hold back his tears and conviction. He was in pain, and it was evident, but you probably would not have noticed it because you kept napping on and off, you thought the service was a little too long. When is enough, enough? God Forbid. Much is required of us. The church is dying, and we must step up or step off. Either you will be the help God wants you to be for the church, or you should just walk away and keep it moving. God is calling for faithful people who are ready to stand up and be true leaders. God holds us accountable when we are out of place. Especially, when you are too busy trying to handle the pastor's job when you are called to be a deacon. You have your own assignment, but you wouldn't know it because you spend too much time trying to do the pastor's job and tell him what to do and what to preach. It is important for us to walk in our own lane and allow God to equip us in our own callings and gifts. The Bible says in the 18th Chapter of Proverbs that a man gifts will make room for him and bring him before great men. In other words, allow God to grow you and empower you for what is to come, and he will begin to open doors for your gifts to be recognized and then elevated. Some of you cannot operate effectively in your assignments because you try so hard to walk in other gifts and callings that you are not gifted in. That is why our churches are broken, confused and without order. People are trying to operate outside of their callings and gifts, and it is not working, and it becomes a total catastrophe. Our service has no anointing and no power anymore. The Praise and Worship team is off spiritually because they are not prayed up and lack power and the evidence of the Holy Ghost.

Ephesians 4: 11-13 (KJV)

And he gave some, apostles, and some prophets; and some, evangelists; and some pastors and teachers; For the perfecting of the saints, for the work of the ministry, for the edifying of the body of Christ: Till we all come in the unity of the faith, and of the knowledge of the Son of God, unto a perfect man, unto the measure of the stature of the fullness of Christ:

Most of the church has lost confidence and trust in our leaders. Because most of us have been torn down and misled by our own leaders who were sent to cover and protect the anointing over our lives but instead our gifts were prostituted or abandoned. Where do we go from here, one may ask? We need to come back to church. We have to put our whole self in and not allow this patty cake praise and worship to be accepted anymore. What is needed in our churches is conviction along with true worship and true praise. There are broken people sitting among us, and they are dying spiritually in our churches all over. These people come to be delivered and set free in our churches, but you judge them and turn up your nose because

67

they don't dress like you. So, they leave because they are too hurt and too embarrassed to stay. Then we complain and talk about it in our church meetings on how the house of God is empty, and people don't want to come to church. We are the ones who are running people out of the house of God because we are so judgmental and hypocritical. Where is the love that God passionately spoke about in the Bible? Love is a fundamental characteristic of who God is. The Bible spoke about the love that God had shown to all mankind. He does not judge us based on race, age, gender, denomination or our ethnic background. God loves everybody, and his love cast out all fear and any form of rejection. That is the same love that we must find in our own hearts. This type of love that God displays is called *agape* in Greek. This love refers to a compassionate and charitable love given to others everywhere and to all mankind.

I want to ask a very sincere question, and I want us church folks to think about it. Where do you go for healing, breakthrough, or deliverance when the church has turned you away?

Please do not continue to read. Let us marinate on this for a moment because this is real and much of the reason why there is a great falling away from God's house. Again, I say, we need to come back to church. Not only bring your body but bring your mind, soul and your spirit. All over the world, people have been deeply wounded and are hurting, and suffering from the pain of being church hurt. This agony has caused many of the saints to fall away from church and become worn and exhausted in the house of God. So, instead of people getting the proper help they need to deal with the pain other things creep in such as Anxiety, Panic Attacks, PTSD, Suicide and Depression. Of course, we don't want to talk about that. That means we have to admit that people are dealing with Mental Illnesses in our churches. Well, it is real, and it is in our churches whether we want to confess it or not. People are suffering and crying out, *silently* for help. The silent cry is because Mental Health Awareness is not talked about among the saints and in our churches and is often frowned upon. Everybody just wants to say *"snap"* out of it. Well, I think if it was that easy most folks would have snapped out of it by now. Others may even say, "Just anoint them with oil they will be alright." You and I both know that God is a healer. There are no questions asked. However, we must also use common sense and not be naïve and hide from the fact that some things need to be dealt with through medication and other substitutes. Well, when will we just *snap* out of it and start talking about it? It is worth the talk. These Mental health concerns are a cry for mental help, and it is my belief they are not going anywhere any time soon.

If you or someone you know is in a crisis and needs immediate help:

- **Call 911 for Emergency Services**
- **Go to the nearest hospital emergency room**
- **Call the toll-free, 24-hour hotline of the National Suicide Prevention Lifeline at 1-800-273-TALK (1-800-273-8255) to be connected to a trained counselor at a suicide crisis center nearest you.**

The problem is that the pastors are too consumed with themselves and who has the biggest church and the most members. We leave the people to fend for themselves because we are just too busy. Instead of seeking help for the people and dealing with the real issues at hand, we level up with titles, tongues and prophecies thinking this will help solve all the problems. Nonetheless, we never get delivered, and we never deal with the pain or get heal from the pain, and the problem only gets worse. It is evident that we can get a fix in church, but could we get healing? This is what God did. He healed the sick and wiped the blinded eyes, and they begin to see. So, tell me again what type of miracles are we performing? The Bible said we should be like him and perform the same miracles Jesus did that we often read about in St. Matthew and St. Luke. But we ask God time and time again to be like him. Which part are we referring to? In order for us to be like him, we must take on a part of him, his glory, the anointing, and his spirit. Some of us are just too narrow-minded and fixated only on self and not what others are need of. You are too busy worrying about what people should be doing for you and not what you could do to help others.

People are struggling and walking around here all broken and bruised, and we are acting like we don't see the bruise or the blood. Some of us are contributing factors of the pain and hurt people are feeling right now. The way we treat each other is so sad, and it breaks my heart to see this type of division among us, the Saints. We have set out goals to hurt each other. We are in competition with our brothers and sisters in Christ. It is no wonder the world frowns upon the church. I am a little sad myself with all the turmoil in our churches. Our mission is to get them before they get me. That is a mindset of the devil, and that is not a mind of God. The Bible tells me to love, for God is love, and we should love one another as God loves us. The question for the today is how can we love God whom we have never seen and see our brothers and sisters in Christ daily and fail to love them. God even calls us a liar, and he says the truth is not in us. It is time out from playing church and misleading and hurting God's people. The church is in a broken state and is in a desperate need of a revival. We have walked away from God and are being tormented by the pressure and agony of this world. Sometimes, being broken can be a place of humility. Oftentimes, that is exactly where God wants us to be so that he can do heart surgery on some of us to uproot the elements that cause deterioration.

God wants us to have peace and harmony in our lives, our church and with one another. We must get back to the basics and visit where the pain first begun and then seek total healing and restoration. It is so disturbing to see so much agony and pain around me that it saddens my spirit. People everywhere are suffering and living in misery but struggling to stay on this side of the ground. Lord, our world needs healing.

2 Chronicles 7:14 (KJV)

If my people, which are called by my name, shall humble themselves, and pray, and seek my face, and turn from their wicked ways; then will I hear from heaven, and will forgive their sin, and will heal their land.

My fervent desire is to see Jesus for myself. I know that it means that I will have to give up some things and allow God to take authority and full control over my life. I am ready for that, and my desire is to let God be my mediator and my keeper and when the enemy comes for me, that God will come for him. Someone helped me the other day when they told me that I could not reach my purpose looking back. They reminded me that God's glory is upon my life, but I must embrace his power within me. I needed to find deliverance and break through the many shackles around my feet that were controlling my path. They also said that I needed to seek total freedom from the strongholds of the enemy that sought out to keep me bound. I was stunned by those words, but it helped me and reminded me that the plans of the enemy are to destroy me and to take me out.

We have to be so careful that we stay under the blood of Jesus and prayed up so that the enemy cannot harm us. The enemy wants to stop us from reaching our destiny. So, he thinks if he can keep us in bondage and oppressed that we will quit the assignment that God has ordained over our lives. The enemy does not care about the anointing that is over your life. Actually, it motivates him to work overtime to hinder the process from going forward. Just know, the enemy does not want you to win and claim the victory in this fight. The plan is for you to get so weary and overwhelmed with life struggles and that you just quit. Well, I don't know about you, but I have breaking news for the enemy, I am not going anywhere. I am in this battle to fight to the finish, and I will not fold. Plus, I am too legit to quit, now. I am fully committed to the Lord with everything that I have, and I have no mind to take down or give up. Yes, I have struggled and labored much along the way with pain and suffering, but I have decided to stay the course and fight the good fight of faith. And, I shall not be moved.

Ephesians 6:12 (KJV)

For we wrestle not against flesh and blood, but against principalities, against powers, against the rulers of the darkness of this world, against spiritual wickedness in high places.

I know that my frustration is with the enemy and his army and not my brothers and sisters in Christ. I know that the enemy does not like the fact that I have sold out to him and have totally made Jesus my choice. The enemy becomes furious and all-out with us when we leave camp and take up our cross to follow Jesus. However, I also need him to know that I will let nothing separate me from the love of God. I will let no thing, and nobody come between and or tamper with the anointing, glory and the power of God that is over my life. I am persuaded that no hurt, no abuse, no broken heart, and no pain and suffering can ever detach me from the love of the father. God is a true healer, and in him, there is no more pain and suffering, hurt and no more brokenness. I am talking about the

Messiah, The Great I Am who has come to take our burdens away. He said to lean on him, and he won't let us fall. We lean on a lot of things for support and for our happiness, and it never lasts. God is saying for us to put our trust in his wonder-working power and allow him to save us and protect us from any backlash of the enemy. You may not have been good and done right by God, but he promised to do right by you. Now, all you have to do is to trust in him and know that he is a Good-Good Father who will never give up on you. He won't let you down like most of our so-called friends who have made several promises to be there, and all we had to do is call. Once we call, they are nowhere to be found. Don't ever think about leaving a message and looking for a returned call because you will be just waiting. You might as well call 911 to a poor neighborhood because they will come quicker than that so-called friend of yours. Aren't you thankful that we have a Father who will not judge us based on our character or our characteristics? He said that we are all his children and are a royal priesthood. He has chosen us from our mother's womb knowing our flaws before we entered this world, but he still said, "she's mine" and "he's mine" without compromise. Oh my, and I say again, what a Good-Good Father.

How many times have you failed God and broken promises? I am ashamed to answer that question and keep my head held high at the same time. I am embarrassed to admit that many of times, not only have I failed him, but I have failed myself. Numerous times, I have let God down by not fulfilling my promises to him, but he has always been faithful to me, and no matter what. Grace, mercy, and favor are the products of God's infinite love for us. They are equal products of the sovereignty of God. But grace and mercy are unmerited and undeserved favor that we cannot earn or buy. It is only given by the grace of God, and it all started at Calvary. Jesus died for our sins and rose on the 3rd day so that we can live again. God owes us nothing but yet continues to give us everything. Now, that is what you call LOVE! It is the LOVE of a Father!

St. John 3:16 (KJV)

For God so loved the world, that he gave his only begotten Son, that whosoever believeth in him should not perish, but have everlasting life.

Chapter Nine

Ye shall not need to fight in this battle: set yourselves, stand ye still, and see
the salvation of the LORD with you, O Judah and Jerusalem: fear not, nor
be dismayed; to morrow go out against them: for the LORD will be with
you.

2 Chronicles 20:17 (KJV)

In the Fight of my Life

Have you ever prayed for strength to stand? I am in that space right
now where I am just asking God for the strength to stand. I am not quite
sure of the season I am in right now in my walk with God, but all I need is
the strength to stand. I believe that I have what it takes on the inside of me
to walk and not be weary, but I am struggling in my faith right now to keep
up the pace and finish strong. Riding to work this morning, the whole
commute, I asked God to help me to stand in this battle I am fighting right
now. I am eager to win this fight and determined to stand as long as the
Lord gives me strength. Lately, I have been in a battle with my mind. You
know how we do, wondering why life steps have taken us in the direction
that we are going and how much longer shall we have to endure the path?
Well, I am not sure of the answers but one thing I do know, if God brings
you to something, he will bring you through it. Even though, I know this, it
is truly hard for me right now. I have seen the ups and downs, good and

bad, and the pretty and the ugly in my life but God has always been faithful and consistent in the midst of it all. So, I cannot waver or give up now. I must stand and fight and not get weary and faint. Most of the time we faint before the battle is over and we never see the finished product or hear the roaring of the crowd. But, today, God is saying for you to stand and not faint. I know the comments on the other side seem discouraging and often can cause you to become fragile but be not weary in your well doing. Your reaping season is around the corner, and God has already supplied all your needs in order for you to succeed in this battle. You are much stronger than your struggles, and God is much bigger than all of your problems.

Psalms 144:1-2 (KJV)

Blessed be the LORD my strength which teacheth my hands to war, and my fingers to fight: My goodness, and my fortress; my high tower, and my deliverer; my shield, and he in whom I trust; who subdueth my people under me.

In this next season of your life, there is no time to waste. You have been given direct orders, and you must follow the instructions prepared for you. All that is set for you to do at this point is wait. That can get frustrating during this time because it causes you to have to trust God when you don't see him. I know that it can be challenging, and I know that you may feel like giving up and walking away but don't, God is molding you and shaping you for your next assignment. This is your time for a complete makeover in him. God is about to change your outlook and perception on the way you view things so that he can get the glory out of everything in your life. Man could not understand it before, but you wait until God has revealed all the things he has in store for you with this next move of God.

Eyes have not seen, nor ears have heard the things that are about to take place in your life following this great transformation.

That is why we have to be willing to wait on God and have patience in our fight. I know it may not look like God is near and fighting for you, but he is, and he is working things out on your behalf as we speak. He is transforming your mind and bringing peace to your heart to condition you. Not only is God restoring your mind, but he is restoring your family's mind and bringing amity where there is war and conflict. I challenge you to stand on God's Word and be not dismayed. God expects for you to win and not lose. He expects you to walk with a winner's attitude. He expects you to speak things that were not as though they were. He expects you to love and live in peace and harmony with our fellow man regardless of the hardship and tough times we may face. God is love. It is God who has always been faithful and true to every word that was ever spoken in my life. I am persuaded, and even in the midst of my struggles, I still remain strong because I am not easily broken or moved.

2 Timothy 1:12-13 (KJV)

For the which cause I also suffer these things: nevertheless I am not ashamed: for I know whom I have believed, and am persuaded that he is able to keep that which I have committed unto him against that day. Hold fast the form of sound words, which thou hast heard of me, in faith and love which is in Christ Jesus.

I know when the going gets tough, the tough gets going. I am often reminded of that during my struggles while it can get depressing along the way, my hope is in the Lord and is built on nothing less. I must keep reminding myself of that truth. It brings clarity and conviction. Although, it can get tough at times, but with the Lord, it gets easier by the passing of the day. So, we must learn to put our trust in God who is the Author and the Finisher of our faith. You have to fight and refuse to be defeated. Do not take down and whimper about the enemy's tactics or his plans. Don't lay there, get up and fight back and give him your best shot. You are already victorious; you just have to move your feet and grab ahold of faith. The enemy only wants to interrogate you and cause you to become fearful and quit. God is your strongest power, and you are not defeated by the enemy or his imps. You cannot allow the enemy to spread lies on you and say that you are not who God has called you to be. For the Word of God says, be ye Holy, for I am Holy. That is who I am, and I will stand on that and that only will I stand. The saying goes, if you don't stand for something, you will fall for anything. Do not be moved!

Never answer to what and who you are not. No matter what the case may be, only answer to what God himself has called you to be. The Bible reminds us that we are a chosen generation and we are peculiar human beings. Since I know that, nobody can tell me otherwise. That is why you cannot answer to anything other than what God has called you. You have to know who you are in God and rest in his care and on his promises. It is important to seek biblical affirmations on your identity in Christ Jesus so that you are reminded of his love for you from the beginning of the creation of the world. Do not answer to the darkness of your past. Most people get caught up in their past mistakes and failures and allow the enemy to order them around and dictate who they are concerning their past. You are not your past, and your past does not define who you are.

Once you can accept that, you will be able to move forward with the plans of God for your own life. The plans of the enemy are to keep you in bondage, living in fear and chained to your past mistakes. You have to outsmart the enemy by owning up to your past and then letting it go. Only revisit it for a testimony but don't dwell there too long or the enemy will try to pull you back to the pit of disgrace and dishonor. I think I shared in an earlier chapter, that you cannot move forward looking backward. You have to see yourself as the Father sees you. You must redeem your ticket of your past and get on board this ship of Zion and ride your troubles away as God heals those broken pieces that are lingering on the inside of you. Now is the time to be set free. There are no more shackles and no more chains. It is time to allow God to finish the work that he has already begun in you. After it is all said and done, let freedom ring. Whom the Son has set free, is free indeed.

The trick of the enemy is to terrorize you and place you into captivity so that you won't find your true purpose. You no longer can be a slave in your own mind. It is time to break free and let this mind be in you that is also in Christ Jesus. You have to see in the spirit and discern what God has already predestined for you. The Bible says to call those things that be not as though they were. You must believe that the path of righteousness has already been made straight for you and all you have to do is clear the runway. The way you do that is get rid of bitterness, jealousy, hatred, pride and other weight that besets you. Just know that once you have repented of your past failures and disappointments, God will forgive you and toss all your sins into the sea of forgetfulness. He does not bring it back up again like your friend around the corner. God will forgive you, and he does not hold it over your head when you do wrong by him. He is a forgiving and loving God who will defend you and hide you in the secret place of the Most High God.

Perhaps, you are struggling with your own past mistakes and failures, and it seems like there is no way out, all you need to do is to connect to the power source, and his name is Jesus. God is saying to you, "Let it go" and "Give it to me and I will give you rest." God has the power to wash away those ugly stains that have tried to contaminate your praise and destroy your destiny. It is time for you to break free, forgive yourself and move on to a better you. This is when God will begin to give you the Peace in your mind that surpasses all understanding. Selah.

Philippians 4:6-7 (KJV)

Be careful for nothing; but in every thing by prayer and supplication with thanksgiving let your requests be made known unto God. And the peace of God, which passeth all understanding, shall keep your hearts and minds through Christ Jesus.

Talking about having to overcome some things in my life, OMG... I have crossed over so many hurdles in my lifetime to the point of some days not knowing whether I was coming or going. I literally did not know the days or the weeks that had passed. I was numbed to life. Most days, I was all over the place in my mind. The enemy's desire was to take my mind and my family. Nonetheless, it was my unwavering faith in God that continued to pull me through every hurdle crossed, and every mountain climbed and for that, To God be the glory! It was my reassurance in the master's plan that allowed me to push beyond the many of setbacks and setups thrown at me day to day. The race has been long and hard and very demanding, but I am still here. Thank you, Lord. The pressure of the pain on the inside has been tough and very overwhelming, but God has kept me sound in my mind. These troublesome times have been hard and very stressful. I have endured a lot of letdowns, hurt and disappointments. Yet, through it all, there is one thing that has always remained consistent, and that is my faith in the Almighty God. I am not where I want to be, but I am thankful, I am not where I use to be. God has been good to me and faithful on every word ever spoken in my life. You see, we have to learn to thank God for the little things and not only that but what he is doing, right now. Sometimes, we wait until the battle is over and then testify, but I believe somebody needs to stop and testify now before the breakthrough, before the deliverance, and before the healing occurs. Somebody needs to shout right now in the midst of cancer, before the result of the Aids test and while you are taking dialysis with the machine drawing your blood and pumping your blood. God is still a healer. You have to believe that and stand on his promises no matter what family or anybody else has to say. I want to encourage you, my faithful reader, who has taken this time out to read this book. This word is just for you, and I want to share it by saying "There is a blessing in the middle of what you are going through." I know it don't look like it because the MRI, the X-Rays and the doctor reports say differently. I know it don't look like it because you didn't get the job interview, your credit score was not high enough, and you were denied the loan, again. I see an open Heaven, and it is just a matter of time for the release of the evidence of your miracles, signs and wonders.

James 1:12 (KJV)

Blessed is the man that endureth temptation: for when he is tried, he shall receive the crown of life, which the Lord hath promised to them that love him.

I am not afraid of the terror by night neither the distractions of the enemy that I face by day because I am leaning on the everlasting arm of our father. All my help comes from the Lord, and I will continue to put my trust in him and lean not on my own understanding. If there is one thing that I do know and that is, God is my Refuge and my Fortress and in him do I trust. I will continue to ask God to build a bridge over the troubled waters that is set before me. However; I will not fear or be afraid because his strength covers me and continues to help me to walk in the midst of the valley shadow of death. I am confident in the Almighty God and the power of his might. My hope is in the Lord and is built on nothing less than his righteousness and by the blood of the Lamb. In Jesus, I know that I am secured because My Redeemer Lives!

Luke 10:19 (KJV)

Behold, I give unto you power to tread on serpents and scorpions, and over all the power of the enemy: and nothing shall by any means hurt you.

Chapter Ten

For the word of God is quick, and powerful, and sharper than any two-edged sword, piercing even to the dividing asunder of soul and spirit, and of the joints and marrow, and is a discerner of the thoughts and intents of the heart.

Hebrews 4:12 (KJV)

It Is Finished

That moment you feel lonely and discouraged, and you burst in tears to the words of this old but familiar hymn...

'Tis so sweet to trust in Jesus,

Just to take Him at His Word

Just to rest upon His promise,

Just to know, "Thus saith the Lord!"

If nothing else, I have learned to rest upon the promises of God. It is by his promise that keeps me holding on to his unchanging hands and waiting in expectancy on the greater that is coming. For I know, it will not always be like this. Also, you should know it won't always be like this. No matter what it may look like in your life or what anyone has to say about the matter at hand, you are much stronger than your struggles. So, weeping may endure for a night, and your faith may even get weaker by midnight, but trust that you have joy coming before the morning break. Sometimes my faith is tested. I am not sure about yours, but I feel defeated sometimes. I know I am not defeated, but I feel defeated.

2 Corinthians 4: 8-9 (KJV)

We are troubled on every side, yet not distressed; we are perplexed, but not in despair, Persecuted, but not forsaken; cast down, but not destroyed.

One night, I was going through, and things began to get rough on every side of the mountain for me. I mean, one problem led to another, and it seemed like it was only getting worse. My faith had collided with fear and frustration. The only strength I thought I had was now down to below zero. I shouted out to my prayer warriors, just in case God wasn't planning to show up by morning. I needed a breakthrough, and I needed it NOW! I told them that I needed them to be on guard and do a *"triple decker"* and **fast and pray** for a miracle by daybreak. I was at my lowest and was not sure whether I had even half of the strength or the faith that I needed to get back on track. I know you may not want to face your truth, but our faith gets weak sometimes, and we fall prey to our weaknesses. This is the way I feel sometimes. Am I alone in this? Is it just me that feels like giving up and calling it quits every other day? So often, life can get confusing, chaotic and very frustrating to say the least, I know. But, even during those moments, we have to be strong in the Lord and rely on his strength to carry us through every obstacle, hurdle or mountain set up to hinder us from moving forward. I am encouraged today, that God has made you and me a promise that he will never leave nor forsake you. It is that promise that continues to keep me near the cross.

Well, to be totally honest with you and since I am a believer, I must admit, there are some days that I want to just let *some* people have it and start wilding out on them because of some of the foolishness and the things they do towards me. Then suddenly, I remember all these things the Bible tells me to do such as forgive and love one another. In one scripture, he warned me and said that I could be angry but sin not. Then I begin to think, if Jesus can take all the things I do against him daily and he still loves and forgive me, I guess, I can do the same for others. Life can be an eye-opener sometimes. All I can say is work on me, Jesus! The enemy thought he had me, but someway and somehow, God pulled me through. I am not where I want to be, but I am not where I use to be either. I am so thankful for life lessons, and one day I will get there with the help of the Lord. I am on my way to heaven land. Won't he do it! I know he can.

Ephesians 3: 16-17 (KJV)

That he would grant you, according to the riches of his glory, to be strengthened with might by his Spirit in the inner man; That Christ may dwell in your hearts by faith; that ye, being rooted and grounded in love.

The Bible says blessed is the man who endureth temptation: for when he is tried, he shall receive the crown of life which is what God has promised each of you. We must learn to hear but not only hear but discern the voice of God so that we can be in tune with him. Without vision, the people will perish. We have to hear what the Spirit is saying to the church. We will be tested and tried by the fire, but we have a choice today to choose Jesus and make him our Savior and Lord Jesus Christ. All we have to do is surrender to his will and allow God to be God in our lives.

Even during my days of solitude, I am equipped to be steadfast and unmoveable, always abounding in the work of the Lord. I am reminded of God's promises to me and his truth which is everlasting, and that report is what I will always believe. Our struggles can sometimes stain our faith and cause us to feel that our situation is doomed and will never change. However, I am convinced that not only will my situation change, but when it is all said and done, I shall have the victory.

I Corinthians 15:58 (KJV)

Therefore, my beloved brethren, be ye stedfast, unmoveable, always abounding in the work of the Lord, forasmuch as ye know that your labour is not in vain in the Lord.

My struggle is just a testament of my faith. If God brought me through before he can definitely do it again. There are some things we have to learn that God will put us through to test our faith and our commitment to him. Oftentimes, God will allow us to be tested with the same test over and over again to refine us and so that we can get to know him more. Our level of assurance to God is more impacted during these times of being tested and tried. Then there comes promotion. Our trials are not to destroy us but to elevate us in God. Without a test, there is no testimony. Occasionally, we are being tested because God wants to bless us and to grow us in him. It may not always be a spiritual blessing or materialistic, but he may want to bless you in your occupation and promote you on a job. The Bible declares if we suffer, we will gain and also reign with him. When we endure hardship and suffering, then we will fully understand what God is doing in and through us. I am fully committed to the cause and to him will I serve through obedience and supplication.

Romans 8:18 (KJV)

For I reckon that the sufferings of this present time are not worthy to be compared with the glory which shall be revealed in us.

We have to be diligent with our assignment and know that the calling on our life is not about us but only to bring God Glory. My mind goes back to all that Paul had gone through with the many trials and tribulations of dealing with the thorn in his flesh. The Bible says 3 times, Paul asked God to allow the thorn to be removed, but God said "No." There are times when God will not co-sign to our weaknesses or our complaints. He will allow us to stay in a place of discomfort just to make us and mold us into warriors in him. It is not always our flesh that needs healing, but our spirit as well. God knew that taking the pain away would not heal the brokenness in Paul. God knew that it was much deeper than what the natural eye could see at the time. He wanted Paul to get the true meaning of being "broken." This thing was spiritual, and Paul needed to see the significance behind him bearing the pain from the thorn that was tormenting his flesh. Only God knows what you and I go through day by day enduring the suffering and pain. He sees our struggles, and he hears our cry. His love is everlasting, and I am blessed today because of his unwavering love for me on that cross that spoke volumes without him ever saying a mumbling word.

James 1: 2-4 (KJV)

My brethren, count it all joy when ye fall into divers temptations; Knowing this, that the trying of your faith worketh patience. But let patience have her perfect work, that ye may be perfect and entire, wanting nothing.

I can attest to you, there is always a mid-term test before the final exam. God has a way of bringing us back to the basics to adjust our lenses in order to ensure accuracy as we move forward in him. Sometimes, we will have to suffer and endure pain and hardships during the process. However, just know, it was all necessary. All we have to do now is trust his leadership and guidance and remember to do all things for the glory of God. Our trials and tribulations only come to strengthen and position us towards a purpose. Oftentimes, our position can be out of alignment and God will have to re-position us so that we can now move in the path of righteousness for his namesake. Remember in the Bible, Zacchaeus climbed up into a Sycamore tree because he wanted to see Jesus?

The Bible says when Jesus came passing through the city of Jericho, people from everywhere came out to see him. My understanding when reading this book, the city was crowded with massive of people standing around waiting on an opportunity to see Jesus. Zacchaeus who was short in statue could not see Jesus because of the crowd of people blocking his path. Zacchaeus could have allowed this to hinder him and make many excuses, but instead, the Bible says that he climbed into a Sycamore tree. I want to pause for a moment to encourage someone who is reading this book. Regardless, of your condition, sometimes you may have to change your position just to get in the face of Jesus. Whatever the case may be, you just have to want it badly enough and go and get it. Zacchaeus wanted Jesus, and he realized that he needed to do something different and re-position himself in order to see him. There are times where we have to fully align ourselves and get in right standing with the Lord so that he can come in and sup with us. This may require changes in our behavior and attitudes and for us to come clean with some things so that God can see our pure motives and intentions.

What was very interesting to me, the Bible declares that Jesus called Zacchaeus by name. You may ask me how Jesus knew Zacchaeus and was able to identify him by name. Well, remember this is the Author and Finisher of our faith whom we are referring to according to the 12th Chapter of Hebrews. Not only does he know your name, but he knows every string of hair that is on your head. He knows all the broken pieces that lie dormant on the inside of you due to fear, frustration, and confusion. He also knows every piece that is disturbed and weakened that has caused you to unfollow him but follow your friends on Facebook, Twitter and Instagram instead. Jesus knows your name, and he wants to accompany you at your home. Are you willing to let him in? I plead with you today. Do not allow your past or failures of your past to cause you to miss your destiny. You have greatness in you. God is bigger than your past, present and your future.

Isaiah 43:1 (KJV)

But now thus saith the LORD that created thee, O Jacob, and he that formed thee, O Israel, Fear not: for I have redeemed thee, I have called thee by thy name; thou art mine.

What you need to pass this test is already birthed on the inside of you. By the way, you are much stronger than your struggles. At this point, the battle has been fought, and the battle has already been won. So, in the words of the Great Messiah, King of Kings and Lord of Lords, **"It Is Finished."**

Author's Bio

Mary Clark Norris, a native of Cairo, Georgia, born to Elder Otis Clark and the late Nancy Clark. The Adopted-Daughter of Bishop Zack and Mary Rogers of Laurinburg, NC. Mary accepted the Lord Jesus Christ as her personal savior and was baptized and filled with the Holy Ghost at the age of 16. While continuing her spiritual journey, the Lord brought Mary to North Carolina where she later joined and served as the Youth President, and sang on the Choir, Praise Team and Ministerial staff at St. John Holiness Church, Laurinburg, North Carolina.

Mary attended Fayetteville State University and majored in Psychology and minored in Sociology. In December 2004, Mary received her Bachelor of Science degree and graduated with honors, Cum Laude in her class. Following her journey to Fayetteville, NC, the Lord then led Mary to Greensboro, NC where she currently resides. Mary later decided to continue her academic studies at North Carolina A&T State University. She graduated and received her Master's Degree in Community Counseling

(Rehabilitation) in December 2010. Mary always knew that the hands of the Lord were upon her life and that God had a great work for her to do. After such a long chastening from the Lord, in July, 2010, Mary accepted and began walking in the call of God to preach the Gospel to God's people. Mary's philosophy on ministry is that her life is a **"living testimony"** to all and she believes that if she can draw souls to Christ through her daily walk; then her living is not in vain. Mary shares often with her friends, colleagues, sisters and brothers in Christ, **"If you are going to talk the talk then it is important to walk the walk."**

Mary is not married and has no children. However; she believes God to be faithful on every Word that he has ever spoken into her life. He may not come when you want him, but he is always on time.

Mary states "One of the greatest joys of being in ministry is eating the **"Word"** first, before delivering the anointed word to God's people". Mary is a songstress, songwriter, and an actress and she enjoys writing songs and poetry. Mary is the author of the books *"When Your Good Aint Good Enough"* and *Speak Life: Ears Have Not Heard.* Mary can be seen in a movie entitled "A Walk to Remember" with major actors such as Mandy Moore, Peter Coyote, Daryl Hannah and Shane West. This movie was written and produced in 2005 by Nicholas Sparks and can be purchased in your local video stores, Red Box and other video settings. Also, watch for local television show times.

Mary enjoys singing and believes in praising the Lord in any atmosphere. As she continues to walk by faith in obedience; destiny and purpose, she shall continue to be fulfilled through the Word of God. Mary understands her journey and believes *"To Whom Much Is Given, Much Is Required!"*

www.ingramcontent.com/pod-product-compliance
Lightning Source LLC
Chambersburg PA
CBHW072205090426
42740CB00012B/2390